A La Mode

A La Mode – The Third Way of Fashion

Editing and design:
Whyart, Aude Lehmann & Tan Waelchli

Authors:
Bastien Aubry, Anus Belkrem, Anuschka Blommers & Niels Schumm,
Julia Born, Dimitri Broquard, Daniela Janser, JOFF, Florian Keller,
Susanne von Ledebur, Aude Lehmann, Cynthia Leung,
Simone Meier, Valerio D'Odorico, David Ratmoko, Shirana Shahbazi,
Zsigmond Toth, Lex Trueb, Tan Waelchli, Tirdad Zolghadr

English translations (Belkrem, Janser, Keller, Ledebur, Lehmann,
Meier, Ratmoko, Waelchli): Peter Routledge
German translations (Leung, Zolghadr): Tan Waelchli
English proofreading: Doris Tranter

Printed by Odermatt, Dallenwil
Bound by Schumacher, Schmitten

Printed in Switzerland

Whyart would like to thank:
All authors, Timo Allemann, Franziska Born, Linda van Deursen,
Barbara Herzog, Urs Lehni, Lucerne University of
Applied Sciences and Arts, Julia Mangisch, Nicole Marsch,
Druckerei Odermatt, Doris Tranter.

Special thanks to Christoph Keller.

Cover image: *Egbert Austin Williams,* 1922
Courtesy of the Library of Congress, LC-USZ62-64931

———

Published by Nieves
www.nievesbooks.com

ISBN 978-3-905714-52-4

A La Mode

The Third Way of Fashion

Whyart

Editorial

'Oh la la, tu es à la mode!' This set phrase might sound flattering on the spur of the moment, but it is not necessarily meant as a compliment. Although fashion can definitely be original and express what amounts to avant-garde individuality, it is much more frequently associated with a commercial industry which in producing numerous copies increases the uniformity of society. Understood in this way, being 'fashionable' really means having *no* style and just going along with things as they are. And in such a view it appears pertinent that 'être à la mode de quelqu'un,' to reconstruct the whole phrase, means to dress in the manner and style of *somebody else.* This always implies failure. You aspire to be a paragon of fashion but in the process you are unable to achieve the very thing you are looking for: originality.

　　Role-Model and imitation, originality and failure. The alternative seems clear from this contrast. Who would not cast themselves on the side of individuality, rejecting industry and commerce? Yet the paradox of fashion is that as 'original' as it might claim to be, it is in fact always already demanding imitation. Since like every avant-garde movement, it works towards a 'coming community,' which would be a community of 'style' and good taste. Seen in this light it makes little sense to hold industry completely responsible for mass market products and to attempt to rescue fashion's bid for originality.

How about starting on the side of imitation instead: attempting to be 'à la mode'? The articles in this book seek out instances of 'fashionable' failures – in film, literature, art, fashion, television and music. What emerges is that failure need not be embarrassing and that it need not in every instance lead to the endorsement of the original model and to uniformity. On the contrary, there are instances where 'à la mode' becomes a principle in its own right, giving rise to novel and selective alternatives which remove the dichotomy between original and copy, and introduce a 'third way' between avant-garde and commercial industry. In the end to be 'à la mode' might no longer mean 'à la mode de quelqu'un,' but 'à la mode de n'importe qui.'

Aude Lehmann & Tan Waelchli

Content

César meets Oscar

At the Museum Shop

Fashion as the Intersection of Art and Life

Tan Waelchli

In contemporary museum shops there are objects which form a strange hybrid of art and fashion: articles of clothing and accessories are decorated with images of works of art. Pollock and Kandinsky silk scarves are on offer in the Guggenheim Museums from Las Vegas to Bilbao, and in the shop which serves both the Louvre and the Musée d'Orsay you can buy ties with motifs of Monet or Van Gogh. Whilst mass tourism obviously takes pleasure in these products, they are regarded by those inside the art world as lacking in taste; a sign of the relentless commercialisation and banality of the art business. But is not this a superficial snap judgement? For if art can be so effortlessly transferred into the commercial sphere, could this not be a sign that the two spheres are much more closely interrelated than we might generally suppose?

One might, for example, call to mind Benjamin's observation in his *Arcades Project* where he noted that artistic 'products' have been 'entering the market as commodities'[1] since the end of the 19th century. He did not mean the art market, but rather he observed that artistic 'forms of construction' had been 'emancipated' from art and produced novel objects which served their purpose as banal capitalist 'commodities.' 'A start is made with architecture as engineered construction. Then comes the reproduction of nature as photography. The creation of fantasy prepares to become practical as commercial art. Literature submits to montage in the feuilleton.' Benjamin was of the opinion that art would not emerge from this development unscathed. He defined works of art as 'ruins of the bourgeoisie' 'shattered' by the 'development of the forces of production'[2], which generated the new commodities. And it was within this context of photography, the graphic arts in advertising, feuilleton etc., that Benjamin also located fashion. In his view fashion was part of the innovative products emerging from the technological 'shattering' of the bourgeois artistic tradition.

It is now still possible in retrospect to re-endorse this appraisal. As does Nancy J.Troy, the art historian, when she draws attention to the way in which famous Parisian fashion designers like Paul Poiret in the early twentieth century had aligned themselves with art. When Poiret stated that what he was creating in his 'studio' through the medium of clothing was a 'portrait' of his clients, his innovative artefacts appeared to transform portrait painting. When he designed costumes for theatrical productions and subsequently sold them as part of his collection, he launched the theatre 'onto the market place as a commodity.' Initially, he also tried to sell a sort of bourgeois exclusivity to his clientele and amongst the methods he employed was the appearance of his wife at theatre premieres as the only person dressed like a stage performer.[3] However, it was in fact here that the problem outlined by Benjamin soon arose. It was evident that the 'development of production processes' meant that large ware-

houses in the USA were beginning to copy Poiret's cre-
ations and if he wished to take action against pirate copies
he had no recourse other than signing license agree-
ments with selected warehouses, thus allowing them to
distribute models in his collection to a mass market.[4]
In this case, the fashion product available off the peg can
thus be described precisely in Benjamin's phrase as a
'monument of the bourgeoisie', now 'shattered.' The transformation of the artistic 'forms of construction' into the
realm of the 'market' – into the clothing sector – finally led
to the destruction of the 'aura' surrounding art because
technology opened the way for reproduction.

What is particularly remarkable about this analysis
is that it also allows us to place within the same context
the innovations brought about by the various modernist
movements. Could it just be coincidental that the modernists rejected the traditional 'forms of artistic creation' at
the very moment they had, as Benjamin observed, 'been
emancipated from art?' And the modernists not only mould-
ed completely new artistic forms, they also redefined
the relationship between works of art and ordinary objects.
Following the maxim 'form follows function,' mundane
objects were no longer supposed to originate from art but
they were to be designed in a simple practical way commensurate with their 'profanity.'

However, the two spheres did not become separate;
on the contrary, they were even more intimately linked, as

is evident from the fact that many artists were also working in the area of design. This new relationship was most aptly described in Nietzsche's concept of 'style.' Regarded as 'communicating' an 'inner tension of pathos through signs,'[5] Nietzsche's concept of 'style' represents the expression of a new artistic experience, starting with the evocation of 'pathos.' This means that the innovative 'stylish' mode designing the world is to be seen as a *consequence* of the innovative brand of art which had introduced a totally fresh experience of pathos. In other words: The new designer objects, which were radically different from the goods produced for a mass market – the debris from the 'bourgeois ruins' – are also an expression of a fundamentally different concept of art.

The avant-garde, or – in Nietzsche's terminology – 'untimely' modernist stance emerged from this fresh perception of art and style. On the one hand, the new kind of artistic experience was supposed to be accessible to all and as such the 'stylish' objects which gave expression to this experience were supposed to be 'reproduced by technology.' On the other hand, the modernists were continually at loggerheads with the limited appreciation by the general public which still clung to its as yet undeveloped, bourgeois concept of art and took pleasure in the capitalist goods it produced. Therefore, although the modernists focused on making an impact on the mass market, they were also extremely elitist and, as a result, the designer objects were produced in very small volumes, or just remained as single items or prototypes. In the meantime, visual reproductions of them were supposed to appear in the mass media – in the hope of exercising a positive influence on public awareness.[6]

Looking back on this project now, it is clear that the modernists have still not succeeded in re-educating the general public. The designer cult continues to be an elitist phenomenon. But it seems that modernism is also wedded to its original aspiration: anybody intending to access a particular niche in post-bourgeois art succeeds in the usual way with an elitist and stylish expression of lifestyle, and it is still vital to disseminate reproductions in the mass media. This particularly applies to contemporary designer fashion, as is evident for example at glamorous events like the Oscars. There for one evening only, the stars wear a highly exclusive item which has been created by a well-known designer, and by stepping on the red carpet they can be transformed by photographers and television into pictures for the mass media. And is not the fashion world generally driven by the logic of producing the ultimate original object? Anybody of any importance will never wear a particular dress on more than one important occasion, and therefore celebrities like Lady Di or Madonna can send their wardrobes to auction from time to time. Here all the details of when and where each dress was worn are divulged. Designer fashion can therefore be seen as an avant-garde artistic counter-movement to the manufactured warehouse collections which had led to the 'ruination' of traditional bourgeois art.

1   Walter Benjamin, *The Arcades Project,* translated by Howard Eiland and Kevin McLaughlin, Cambridge, MA: Belknap 1999, p. 13.

2   Benjamin, *Arcades Project,* p. 13.

3   Cf. Nancy J. Troy, *Couture Culture: A Study in Modern Art and Fashion,* Cambridge MA: The MIT Press 2003, p. 51, p. 209.

4   Cf. Troy, *Couture Culture,* p. 269.

5   Friedrich Nietzsche, *Ecce Homo: How To Become What You Are,* translated by Duncan Large, Oxford: Oxford UP 2007, p. 40.

6   Cf. Beatriz Colomina, *Privacy and Publicity: Architecture as Mass Media,* Princeton: Princeton UP 1993.

Greetings from Bilbao

Clothes Aude Lehmann
Photography Zsigmond Toth
Styling Philipp Junker

Model Noreen Carmody /
option models
Hair Tanya Koch / b4 agency
Make up Nicola Fischer /
style-council
Photographic assistance
Julia Mangisch, Toby Buehler

The collection 'Greetings from
Bilbao' was made in collaboration
with Franziska Born.

p. 18 / p. 28: Gilet by Vivienne
Westwood Anglomania; shoes
by Yves Saint Laurent;
hat, stylists own.
p. 21: Necklace by John Galliano
p. 23: Jacket by Junya Watanabe
for Comme des Garçons
p. 27: Stockings by Fogal

Why Roger Buergel Wears Red Jeans

Notes on Freedom of Choice

Tirdad Zolghadr

So Roger Buergel, director of the 2007 Documenta, wears red jeans. A light scarlet type of red, the kind of jeans you find in sociology departments in Germany and countryside discotheques in Holland. On other occasions he wears balloony trousers of black tunic, and as he walks up to the speaker's panel he pulls up the elastic strap around his waist, forming a cute little hackey-sack blob at the crotch. *Sehr menschlich*, as the Germans would say.

Now remember Okwui. Okwui Enwezor dresses impeccably; shirts by Richard James, loafers by Gucci, and he speaks in theoretical pictograms and academic metonymies, debunking metadiscourses and terrifying conference interlocutors with his pirouettes as he goes along. Buergel, by contrast, sounds like a Berlin student on a Cuban Solidarity package tour, smoking Beedees round the campfire, talking about 'common psychic experiences,' refering to Enwezor's shows as 'zoos,' and scoffing at 'sensationalism.'

Beedees or Davidoff. I once read in an historical encyclopedia that Nikita Khrustchew indulged in a favorite party game in which everyone at the table was obliged to partake, at odd hours of the night, after many rounds of Vodka orange. It was called *La question qui tue*, or The Big Question. It consisted of little more than offering two impossible options to choose from, like Pelmeni or Bliny. Pushkin or Dostojewsky. Painting or photography. Screwdriver or Bloody Mary. Gucci or Prada. Christian Boltanski or Ilja Kabakov. Friends of mine picked up on this several years ago, and, since then, the game has proved its potential to unmask unsuspected ideologies in your closest colleagues, to sow strife and anger among romantic couples, and to poison any dinner party with gratuitous polarization.

The intriguing thing here is the allegorical thrust of a question like, say, Britney or Amy, Hillary or Barack, Shahrzad or Whyart; it renders the choice between bad and worse something exciting, stimulating, even pleasurable. This is because once the autonomous subject, the interviewee, has opted for the one, and not the other, these shades of sameness, already cast as binaries in the question, are once again transfigured into colossal oppositions in the answer, since the most subtle rhetorical devices must be employed to defend the 'choice' at hand.

These concoctions of contrast between largely congruent figures touch upon the construction of Free Choice as an ideological device in the many little distinction games that mark the habitus of any arts professional. Games of the kind need to be all the artful in what some call an era of 'post-medium-specificity,' an era where any artistic medium (or political style or fashion statement) is up for tactical abuse and strategic regurgitation, rather than enjoying the auspices of a hallowed history of a particular intellectual tradition, the way, say, the medium of painting did until recently. In a situation where any qualitative consensus is grimly undermined – due to a surprisingly broad consensus that any broad consensus must be grimly undermined, lest we all degenerate into a screaming horde of fascist hyena pigs – it's harder and more challenging to make Choices with the poise of an edict.

The promise of entertainment and direction and Sound and Fury aside, the ideology of Free Choice conceals how limited our professional margins really are, circumscribed by peer groups, personal vanities, language skills, EU funding policies, class background, e-flux, perennial aesthetic ideologies and airline tariffs. Istanbul or Berlin, Sharjah or Singapore. The sheer routine of pursuing art as a job drives curators and critics to dramatize their choices even when they're merely formulaic compromises, and thrust them upon the audience as the dangerous pursuits of a radical Third Way – 'NO to aestheticism, and NO to the dogma of political activism – *I say we need BOTH aesthetics and politics!!!!*' At other times, the critic adamantly, furiously, grimly refuses to choose, hovering somewhere along the symmetric middle in exquisite critical dilemma – 'Revolution is dead and liberalism means compromise – *what to do now!!!!*'

Tristesse Royale or *No Pasaran*. Critical temperament in the art scene is still imbued with the sad melancholia of impossible choices, or the honorable responsibility of the Right Ones. It's closer to Don Quixote's universe of chivalry than the global village square in which we are supposed to live.

– *Mono or stereo ?*

Cross-dressing Class

The Imposter as an Artist of Travesty

Florian Keller

Zelig, Woody Allen, USA 1983
Film stills (details)

The thumb of his right hand is tucked casually into his jeans pocket; absorbed in thought he scratches his chin with his other hand. He casts an innocent glance sideways, perhaps shyly or incredulously. And the red signature on the label: *Pepe Jeans, London* straddles his stomach. Another picture shows him in a similar dreamy but self-assured pose; this time with bare torso and arms covered with the red signature of the label: *Emporio Armani.* Finally, we see him once more, still with bare torso, but now directing a provocative glance towards the onlooker. Above his upper arm there is an illustration of a flacon and beneath it is the white label signed *Gucci.* So this beautiful young man, the 'Gucci imposter,' was destined for a few days at least to be a national celebrity.

Having put it together himself, the 25 year old Juan Isidro Casilla flogged the Gucci advertisement in February 2007 to a free Swiss newspaper; two days later he even achieved a double-page insert in the broadsheet, the *Sonntagszeitung.* Two months earlier he had made a very glossy appearance as a phoney Armani model in a Swiss magazine without anybody suspecting anything. Only the gay publication on which he had already tried to palm off his jeans advert politely turned him down. The financial damage which Casilla wreaked with his forged adverts was put at 100,000 franks. The theoretical 'surplus value' which this has generated is encapsulated in the following assertion: the persona of the imposter provides the perfect subject for fashion.

As a repeat offender, the imposter realises the ideal and aspiration of fashion: every new garment which we wear should make us what we want to be: 'Create yourself! Carry on recreating yourself!' The imposter takes fashion's magic charm with its subjective poetic connotation quite literally. And like fashion he needs the spotlight to enable him to shine; he plays out his role in the full gaze of the public because the twilight is not bright enough for him.

The imposter is not a compulsive deceiver. He always flouts social conventions but not necessarily the law. From his earliest origins he has defined himself primarily by his look which makes more of him than he is. When the term *imposter* first emerges in the eighteenth century it refers to beggars who rise above their social status by dressing in such a way that they acquire an outward air of distinction. A term springs to mind from *Queer Theory*: the imposter is a *cross-dresser,* whose theatrical roles cover the whole social range. His show might then be called *Cross-dressing Class.* It is a travesty which has less to do with sexual identity than with the indicators of social differences.

Woody Allen devised what was surely the greatest of these virtuoso roles in a film in which he raises the imposter's role to an art form. In *Zelig*, his spoof documentary film (USA 1983), he invents an everyman figure called Leonard Zelig (played by Allen himself). Haunting the twentieth century as an inconspicuous conformist, Zelig constantly adapts to the particular social milieu of the time by dint of his astounding powers of mimicry. Con-

fronted with gangsters he becomes a gangster; amongst rabbis he becomes a rabbi; with Nazis he is a Nazi.

Zelig, the 'human chameleon' is a radical fashion phantom: being both the perfect conformist, and at the same time always novel and elusive, he embodies the fundamental paradox of fashion. The inner conflict leads to an ironical climax when at the end of the film, having been cured of his pathological tendency to adaptation, Zelig develops his own personality in America. By assuming American identity in such an exemplary manner after his therapy, Zelig has in fact merely conformed to the predominant pattern of life once more. That is the impenetrable tragedy which reverberates throughout Woody Allen's film. Although subjected to the healing process, Zelig remains a chameleon when, finally like any good American, he has learned to express his opinions and say what he thinks.

From the nobody who poses as a model, to the beggar who takes on the role of the nobleman and the human chameleon called Zelig, the imposter as *cross-dresser* undermines the codes which determine affiliations to a particular social group. Steven Spielberg's film *Catch Me If You Can* (USA 2002) exemplifies the importance of dress code and traces the escapades of a real imposter who passes fraudulent cheques. Leonardo Di Caprio plays Frank William Abagnale Jr., who so fired the public imagination in the late '60s that he was soon given the nickname 'James Bond of the skies' for his adventures as a phoney pilot. Whilst still at school and without instruction, he acquires the uniform of a Pan American Airways pilot – and from that moment on, when dressed in the symbolic fabric he *is* a pilot because he is recognised as such.

The uniform, as service dress, is to some extent the antithesis of the individual aspirations generated by fashion. A pilot's uniform may be perceived as a non-conformist fashion statement in a disco or on the catwalk, but in the context of air travel it is a statutory requirement. When the hero in *Catch Me If You Can* contrives his unauthorised promotion, this neverthless makes clear that as an imposter he has internalized the fundamental paradox which fashion creates between the avant-garde and mass culture. The uniform in fact singles him out as a mere impersonator aspiring to the mundane image of a pilot; yet it is this same uniform which enables him to realise fashion's greatest desire: to become a splendid creation of oneself. Conversely, this means that his extravagance is always well adapted. His life depends on his paradoxical and outstanding gift for adaptation. And just at the point when his talent is recognised he is relegated to what in reality he is: a phoney who tries to be something more than he is.

Spielberg's film is particularly interesting because he emphasises what was already indicated by Woody Allen: that the imposter pragmatically fulfils the American dream. When the fortunes of Abagnale's bourgeois family and his parents' home fall apart – a tax dispute having precipitated

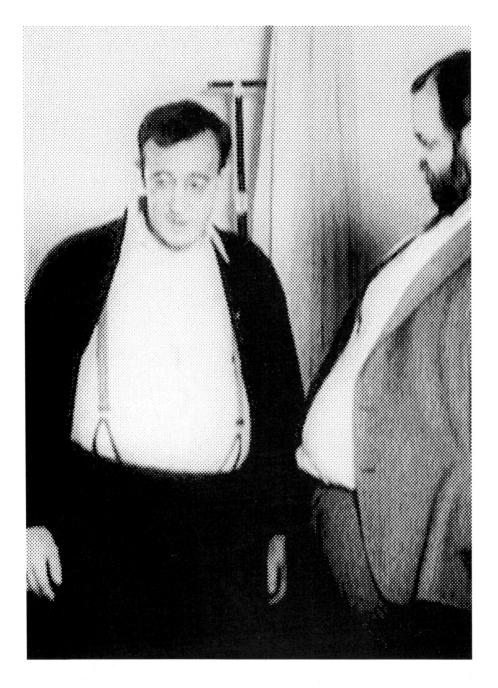

his father's ruin – the son obtains justice and offsets this social debacle by fulfilling the dream of success on his father's behalf. He achieves material prosperity by passing off fraudulent cheques, and as a phoney doctor, pilot and lawyer he equips himself with the symbolic capital necessary for high society. That is how the young hero in *Catch Me If You Can* is able to change into his personal reality the very fiction which is supposed to be maintained by the American dream: the myth which affirms the idea of unlimited social mobility.

Although class structure in America has not disappeared, it is allegedly more fluid than anywhere else in the world. The spirit of the Constitution is such that success and social advancement are equally open to all. As shown by the hero in Spielberg's film, this aspiration can easily be interpreted as an invitation to imposture. The imposter's aim is to overcome social divisions by role play – the American dream is about something very similar. Or to put it more pointedly: the American dream is a collective phantasy which transforms the way in which the imposter projects himself into an expectation of success shared by all.

The hero from the title of F. Scott Fitzgerald's *The Great Gatsby* (1925) is a shining example and his tragic end is a reminder of the dark side of this phantasy. Anybody like Jay Gatsby who relies on the American expectation of the 'good life' is dependent, in his pursuit of happiness, on the possibility of suddenly having to abandon the past in order to rediscover himself. *You can find happiness by being someone else,* that is the fascinating formula which Frank Rich, the cultural critic has coined for the American dream. It is the imposter's maxim, which has been rejigged as a national myth of success.

Perhaps it is not coincidental that the greatest literary inventor of America on European soil was Karl May, a convicted imposter who was said to deck himself out with the biographical details of his invention, Old Shatterhand. Karl May provided his own photographic evidence when he was snapped in the full rig of a Western hero – the writer as the male model for his own literary phantasies.

'I'm nothing, really,' says the hero of himself in *Catch Me If You Can* on one occasion. That is the withering suspicion from which fashion and the American dream seek to release us. But the imposter is alone in seeing the infinite possibilities which this sad self-appraisal opens up: *I'm nothing, really. Let's dress up!*

Don't Mock the Clothes!

The Modish Existentialism of
Sex and the City

Simone Meier

Once upon a time there was the most wonderful television series in the whole world. It had the most beautiful clothes, many beautiful people, exquisite locations and terrific dialogues. Cheeky, sexy, fast and stylish. It was the glamorous rock version of a TV series. Called *Sex and the City,* it was all about four heterosexual single women in New York, Carrie, Samantha, Charlotte and Miranda, who had been specifically designed by homosexuals. Written by a gay, Darren Starr, it was staged by Patricia Field, a lesbian. And nearly every woman in the world without exception could identify with some aspect of it.

Thus subculture had discovered a magic mirror reflecting the mainstream and it slotted a dream into it which everybody suddenly wanted to live out. This dream is about the emancipated, professionally successful, sexually active, financially independent and extremely attractive urban single woman; she has her life sufficiently under control so that both she and it can be seen as vehicles for desirable, antique, or simply light-hearted, beautiful fashion items or accessories. Fashion seen as a metaphor for a modern girl's life; fashion as a driving force for a television series which achieved success worldwide; fashion as the indicator of increased globalisation. All this is encapsulated in the global cachet of the luxury labels which at least the protagonist of *Sex and the City,* the blond agony aunt, Carrie Bradshaw would never have been able to afford in real life if the series had been a realistic portrayal of the average professional New York woman.

But realism was not the issue here. The main concentration was on actual desires which in this series, as if in a fairy tale, were constantly fulfilled. It was no longer a question of: will the woman find her prince? But will she find her male accessory and now, before that will she succeed in bagging (and paying on her own) for the new Fendi handbag or the new Manolo Blahniks? And every woman in the world understood *Sex and the City,* for names like Prada, Dolce, Chanel, Dior and Fendi were meaningful to them as these particular stores have been in every large city for some time, much longer than the egalitarian stores like H&M or Ikea and often much longer than the internet. Such labels were already benefiting from globalisation before anybody had even heard of the word. A simile like: 'Clooney is like a Chanel suit. He'll always be in style' (Samantha) or 'My marriage is a fake Fendi' (Charlotte) is immediately understood everywhere. And nothing is more catchy than 'A relationship is like couture. If it doesn't fit perfectly, it's a disaster.' (Samantha)

Surprisingly, nobody in this field raises any concerns about global uniformity. The best illustration of this is Ermenegildo Zegna, the Italian menswear luxury label which for many years featured Adrien Brody in its advertising and made a name for itself in the winter of 2007 with the slogan 'great minds think alike.' And they dress alike. It is impossible not to comply. The exclusive uniformity is chic and every item of clothing coming within this category is automatically integral to one's personality; when wearing it there is a great emotional bond. 'Don't mock the clothes,' Carrie reprimands an unreasonable lover. 'Swear on Chanel,' she demands from the same man when he is forced to keep a secret. People are fallible. Fashion is not. A dress is what it is: beautiful and perfect in every respect, nothing more nor less. This could be seen as the light-hearted catwalk variation of existentialism.

In *Sex and the City,* the language of fashion signifies a feminine world where people are reduced to objects and there is an absence of sentimentality, but aesthetic qualities survive. Sometimes this even works almost without label-dropping. 'A squirrel is just a rat with a cuter outfit. City girls are just country girls with cuter outfits,' Carrie concludes after an unhappy visit to the country. Samantha's confession 'I'm a lesbian' – a remark limited to very few episodes – is followed by the redheaded Miranda's 'I am a fire hydrant.' To clarify the issue Samantha has to add that sexual orientation is just 'a label, like Gucci or Versace.'

The climax of the existentialism of fashion occurs in the series when Carrie takes part in a fashion show. The episode is called *The Real Me* and Carrie, wearing glittering briefs designed by Dolce & Gabbana, finds her real ego on the catwalk, flanked by well known amateur models like Frank Rich, the columnist of the *New York Times* and the authentic Heidi Klum. It is a self-confident, stronger, more glamorous, tongue-in-cheek triumphant ego, which gets up again after an embarrassing fall on the catwalk and outdoes everybody with her performance. A proud image of feminine self-empowerment. And like all the costumes in *Sex and the City* the glittering briefs may well have seen their second spring in Patricia Field's vintage boutique in Manhattan. It was Field who made an utter fortune from selling luxurious, flimsy dresses formerly worn by actresses.

Only when faced with creation itself are there any signs of fashion's limitations. A few episodes after Carries' catwalk triumph, Miranda's waters break like a hydrant, when about to give birth she wets Carries' Cinderella shoes embellished with pink tulle; they are the most expensive ever. 'And thus, with a destroyed pair of Christian Louboutins, began Miranda's delivery,' we hear Carrie saying off stage. And we are happy that something so profane as waters breaking can now be associated with a highly prestigious label.

Viktor & Rolf, I Love You (Almost)

Cynthia Leung

Dear You,

You kind of fucked up, didn't you? Should I be more generous and say that *we* fucked up? The second I want to scream I HATE YOU, I arm myself with the perfect vision of a Viktor & Rolf dress: a billowing gown with I LOVE YOU splashed across it, a celebration of shamelessness over sadness.

It was spontaneous and it felt right. I asked for your hand in marriage: Should we? Do you want? You said yes. On a beach in Hong Kong after a friend's wedding. It could not have been more postcard romantic than that – how deliciously cliché of me. I was wearing a white, knotted Helmut Lang summer dress and feeling brazen. Forty years from now, I might say this was when I looked the most beautiful.

You claimed that in fact, you had thought about asking me the same question the day before, as we trekked through the tropical jungle in the dark. We had given up on reaching my favorite beach because the sun had run down. So we turned back to civilization. I remember the retreat, backtracking by the glow of our cell phones, the shadows creating a romantic fear. How ladylike of me to grab your hand tighter in the dark, my tiny sign of vulnerability.

No matter. After Sophia's wedding, I took it into my own hands, and you said yes. So what if we were high?

The next morning, I didn't regret a thing. And neither (you said), did you.

From there, it was a small series of announcements, amongst friends and family. We flew to Spain and scouted a gilded church, a bearded priest, and a modest lighthouse at the Eastern-most tip of the country, where Salvador Dali and Gala had built their insane love shack by the sea. There was the letter we scripted to the British owner of the lighthouse: Would he be so kind to let us hold our wedding celebration there? When he laughed, 'Everyone thinks their love is special,' and asked for more money, we thought, what a jerk ... but secretly, the brakes were being applied, from this moment on.

What better way to smooth over this glitch than to focus on the costume? Secretly for me, there was the question of the dress. I'm not a princess. I'd never harbored a wedding dream or a fantasy gown. Yet here was a new challenge: to envision a costume to embody a forever-in-a-day. To be dressed in the ultimate symbol of our love, to prove to a callous world – and to that Jerk Lighthouse Brit – that I would choose love over hate.

Still, I never shared this fantasy outfit with you. I was embarrassed to admit its existence aloud. But you're vain. So you need to hear it. It's all coming out now, like your dirty laundry that unexpectedly spilled into mine.

There were a few candidates. There was a 1940s wedding gown that I had picked up in a California thrift shop

years ago, only because it was a bargain. Maybe I could
sell it on eBay, I thought, to some pretty blonde lady
happy with its shiny satin, its puffed sleeves, the tiny but-
tons and elaborate lace train. Maybe she was an older
bride welcoming her second trek to the altar, someone will-
ing to embrace her embattled past? You wouldn't want to
see me this way, and neither did I.

And so there was a new vision of Elsa Schiaparelli's
Lobster Dress, a clever and appropriate Surrealist statement for the occasion, of marriage being surreal. For one
day, I could be a lobster by the sea, in Spain. Red, ready
to be caught, ugly claws and all. I soon discovered that un-
less I was a powerful curator at the Met's Costume Insti-
tute, or a distant Schiaparelli relative, it was out of reach.
The Lobster Dress lives only in a vitrine.

That's when I thought of Viktor & Rolf. Forget history,
I concluded. What I needed was Fantastic Designer, and a
few dollars to afford the luxury. And that became part of
our arguments, a tiny tear. Perhaps I spent more on designer shoes than on dinners with you.

Later on, when you insisted that I too had lied in our
relationship, you pointed out the day when I shot out of
bed and announced that I was going to work early, at 7:00
am. Instead, by 7:30 am I was in line at H&M in Soho,
so excited to inhale Viktor & Rolf's collection for the masses.
I admit I was curious about their ironic wedding dresses
quietly hanging by the entrance.

Surrounded by pandemonium, eyeing the dress rack, it seemed wrong, like a shotgun wedding in the outskirts of Las Vegas: a sad statement that, a la Britney Spears, you could easily back out of the deal. What I dragged home instead was a tuxedo, and silently, you immediately sensed my little white lie. *Liar, liar, pants on fire.*

It became comical. And finally I remembered Viktor & Rolf's joke of a gown, a wedding gown made for a drag queen. I could be this absurd confection. Not really a dress, more a scenario: like a child had grasped a red crayon and in a fit of giggles, scrawled 'I Love You' on her bed sheets and then wrapped it on her body like a primitive toga. Just for fun, playing grown up, for no one in particular. It could have been an exuberant fuck you to the lighthouse owner, or now, as I now see it, a white flag – the last gasp… can't you see? I LOVE YOU.

I imagined what it would be like to try on the dress, to navigate its interior. I felt the weight of heavy layers of silk duchesse satin, the brief claustrophobia when confused of the way in, where to put the right arm, the left, ducking in the head with eyes closed. I could feel the tentative sucking in of air, a tensing of the stomach, wondering how it would fit, the process of taking it off, to make the inevitable escape.

I even sat with Viktor and Rolf themselves in the lounge of a depressing American department store and learned that in fact, the dress I'd long fantasized about belongs to

Celine Dion! It's probably hanging in Celine's closet in Las Vegas, totally untouched – cue the *Titanic* theme song, please.

Knowing you, you think it's inelegant, this pathetic dress talk. What is there to prove in our relationship anymore, except to examine its empty corpse? Guess I can still try it on and speak about it from within, to show you its series of confusing tunnels, of false pockets of security, of seams secretly coming apart, the layers and layers of tulle holding up a surface that slowly deflated and finally, collapsed. You could sense it too, right? Or were you just thinking of renting a tuxedo?

Wherever you are, I'm glad we didn't make it. I'm happy that *I* asked *you* first. I don't think about the failure of us anymore, but sometimes I do think about that outrageous Viktor & Rolf gown, missing a body to give shape to I LOVE YOU. Just a floating ghost, an empty promise I tried on in my mind. It was never mine, so now it's all the easier to let go. I ... forgive you.

Goodbye,

Miss C. Havisham

Daylight

Photography
Shirana Shahbazi

Dual Form

A Plea for the Model

Anus Belkrem

As a well-known hair stylist with a large clientele, drawn from fashion, film and the arts, I am often invited to private views. I nearly always go along as I do need to keep in touch, but often feel rather perplexed when contemplating the work on display. It is because a work of art does not have to look particularly good and, therefore, you cannot just tell by looking at it whether it is good or bad. The main criterion for determining its quality seems to be hidden. Although you see the form, you do not see the content.

Most people rely on outside help to understand the content; for example, they turn toward the specialists who write for art catalogues. These guys seem to know what it is that is hidden and they are able to interpret the work. But I never read these extracts. They remind me of the 'making of' features about big movies, and I can never imagine anybody wanting to look at such things. It is just like a magician who reveals his tricks to you at the end of his performance. And the same it is with the work of art and its content.

Things are easier in fashion. Fashion does not have a deeper meaning; it just has to look good. It has no not-able theory and we can be thankful for that. In fashion the garment is the form and the person wearing it is the con-tent. Thus unlike in art, both form and content are visible.

The person wearing the garment is, first and foremost, the model presenting the collection. The utmost attention is given when choosing a model and this is absolutely right because the content is all important. But a new problem emerges: generally what is required in a model is the ulti-mate ideal form. (Many experiments have already been carried out in which very small, disabled or elderly people were sent onto the catwalk, but this does not work, and it is not difficult to see why.) And this quest for a good form which is clearly defined (specific length, height, width) results in the content becoming vague.

Therefore, one might be forced to conclude that fashion works without any kind of content. The model, ap-pearing at first glance to be the content, is also strictly following the principle of good form, so that a sort of dual form emerges. And because the model really cannot do anything apart from looking good (if he/she could sing, per-form or dance, they would do just that), it is difficult to endow fashion with any sort of content. To be honest, I pre-fer no content at all to something hidden.

– This world is really fucked up

The Kate Show

Johnny Cash
Delia's Gone, 1994

The Icon Between Portrait and Model

Aude Lehmann & Tan Waelchli

Inez van Lamsweerde/
Vinoodh Matadin, 2005

In the autumn of 2006 Olivier Zahm curated 'The Kate Show,' an exhibition about Kate Moss, held in the Museum of Photography (foam) in Amsterdam. Alongside the work of fashion photographers – Juergen Teller, Inez van Lamsweerde, Terry Richardson etc. – the work of artists who had featured Kate was also on show, e.g. Richard Prince, Andro Wekua a.o. As a result the supermodel appeared as a figure who is equally at home in art and fashion and it was in this context that Zahm spoke of an 'icon.' He went on to say that he was interested in the 'tragedy which the production of the icon represents for both the people who distance themselves from it and for those living in its light.'[1]

Terry Richardson, 2006

Andro Wekua, 2006

80

What does this definition imply? If Zahm locates the icon in both art and fashion then it is to be seen as intersecting the two spheres. And this could serve as a reminder that art and fashion are normally separated: a work of art is original whilst a fashion picture in magazines or on posters is reproduced by technology. There is also a considerable difference in content: although images in art and fashion frequently look similar, particularly where portraits are concerned, in art the emphasis is on people, whereas in fashion it is on clothes.

Artistic portraits follow certain conventions of portraiture. People are depicted in typical settings; they are endowed with suitably representative clothing and status symbols and staged in set poses. The effect is that the people illustrated in this way approximate to a certain ideal; an attempt might even be made to perfect their facial characteristics.

But within this context it is accepted that the individual characteristics of each person should ultimately be left intact: indications as to age, profession, particular facial features or a certain look. This brings about a tension between the conventional image and the person portrayed. Their individuality is never completely caught up in the ideal – not even in nude painting because individual physical features, unusual proportions and prominent wrinkles etc. are always evident.

Francisco Goya,
*Dona Teresa
Sureda,* 1805

Jacques-Louis David,
*Madame de
Verninac,* 1799

Paul Cézanne,
*Woman in a
Red-Striped
dress,* 1892–96

Vincent van Gogh,
La Mousme, 1888

Raphael,
*Portrait of a Nude
Woman,* 1518

Pablo Picasso,
*Woman Sitting
Nude,* 1905

In fashion, on the other hand, clothes are the main focus. They are to be seen as prototypes which are offered to an as yet undefined clientele. The model embodies this generality. It represents as it were a virtual ideal, and therefore individual traits of personality must not be given any consideration. In addition, the model must be able to switch into various roles – corresponding to the clothes being worn at that particular moment. Its hallmark is the complete art of being able to change, yet always remaining itself, the model.

The antithesis becomes clear if you compare two extremes. An artist like Lucian Freud pays so much attention to people's individual characteristics, that we only see individuals with their 'faults' and almost forget the underlying ideal. Helmut Newton, the fashion photographer, on the other hand, places such clear emphasis on the virtual ideal that the models are in danger of losing all their humanity and almost looking like dummies in a shop window.

Helmut Newton,
Les nus et les vêtus,
Vogue (France) 1981

Lucian Freud,
Double Portrait, 1988

Lucian Freud,
Naked Girl Asleep, 1968

84

Assuming that there is this distinction between art and fashion, how should we define that junction where the iconic Kate is located? Kate became famous in the early '90s at a time when a new kind of fashion photography was being developed in magazines like *ID, The Face* etc. The pictures were supposed to look less doll-like than previously, more ordinary; and sometimes the photographers went so far as to depict ordinary people from off the street in their own clothes. In this environment and thanks to photos by Corinne Day or Juergen Teller a.o., Kate could aspire to be representative of the new style, because she looks very special as a model. For example, she is smaller than is normally specified – but she has that 'special something.'

Corinne Day, 1990   Juergen Teller, 1994

Kate became so famous with a face which was 'not quite ideal' but 'somehow special' that she avoided changing into a doll, even after she had become a much sought after model for traditional fashion photography (which resulted largely from the advertising for Calvin Klein Underwear). Despite all efforts made to present Kate as a model, we continue to recognise her – even in a Helmut Newton picture.

Helmut Newton, 1992

Therefore, Kate is never totally part of the fashion scene. Although she, like other models, epitomises the virtual ideal, she does so without becoming faceless and turning into a doll. She manages to preserve her individuality and thus achieves something which normally only happens in art. However what distinguishes her from the typical object of artistic portraiture is that her specific characteristics do not appear as a 'flawed' deviation from an underlying ideal. On the contrary, Kate seems paradoxically to epitomise the ideal by virtue of her *particular characteristics*. She does remain an individual but *as such* she also comes across as the virtual 'model' of fashion photography.

Lucian Freud, 1992

Marc Quinn, 1992

Taking this paradoxical correspondence between the particular and the ideal as a definition of the icon, it is reminiscent of the original meaning of that concept. Icons were originally those saints who by virtue of their exemplary lives had reached the same status as Christ: they had become 'images of God.' Here the same principle that distinguishes the 'icon' Kate came to apply, namely, that the virtual ideal was encapsulated in a particular person.

Moreover, tracing the icon back to the concept of the 'image of god' reveals one of its more surprising features: it shows that a person who has become an icon no longer exists 'behind' their picture, but rather such a person *is* the very icon, the 'image of god.' This identity of image and

person is also a problem for a contemporary icon like Kate, as the photographs taken by paparazzi make evident. They try to show Kate as an ordinary person 'behind' the 'virtual' pictures, and that is why they are particularly interested in scandals which are intended to reveal that she too is a flawed human being. But this attack on what is assumed to be the model's 'false' image fails. Even when Kate is shown sniffing cocaine we are not able to see in her anything other than the icon which we have learned to love in the fashion magazines. Kate remains Kate, whether it be in art, in fashion or in the photos taken by the paparazzi.

1   'The Magazine is Fashion', in: Christoph Doswald (Editor), *Double-Face,* Zurich: JRP|Ringier 2006, p.95.

'Ofoffjoff – One to One – Offshoot' is a sequel
project to 'Ofoffjoff – One to One,' a publication by
JOFF and Julia Born, which was itself a sequel
project to 'Ofoffjoff,' JOFF's one-off collection presented during the fall 2005 fashion week in New
York. The collection consisted of 10 outfits, all
made on the designer's own size and produced in
highly limited editions, which were sold to fans
and collectors right after the performance, letting
them aspire to become part of what they just saw.
This idea of opening up the unique and surreal
world of the model to 'real' fashion customers was
further examined with 'One to One.' JOFF and
Julia Born asked Anuschka Blommers and Niels
Schumm and to take pictures of the collection
with JOFF as the model, and then composed a
book by reproducing the 10 photographs in life-
size scale, so that now everyone who would buy
the posters could wear the clothes – except that
they were mere copies, made of paper... How
such a proliferation might look is explored in 'Offshoot,' another photo work by Blommers/Schumm,
which shows JOFF 'dressed' in the posters. With
the 'real' JOFF thus entering the surreal world of
the fashion spread, it seems as if reality itself
became surreal.

Ofoffjoff
One to One
Offshoot

JOFF & Julia Born

Photography
Anuschka Blommers & Niels Schumm

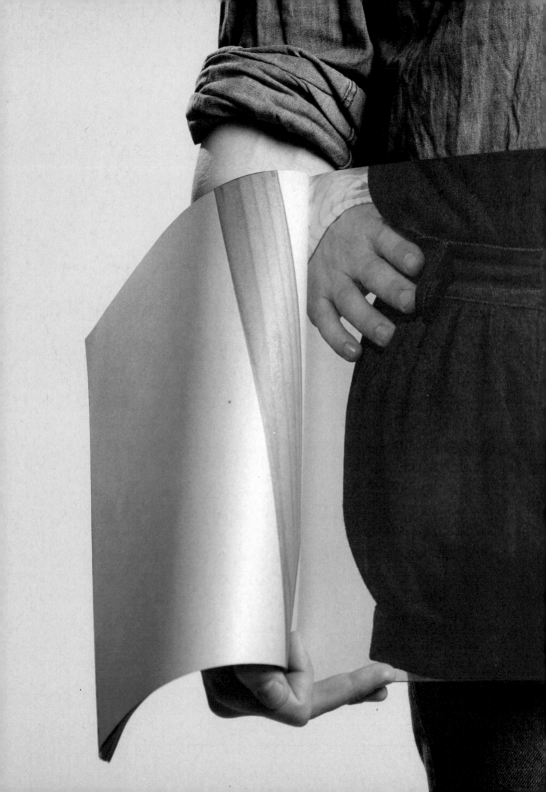

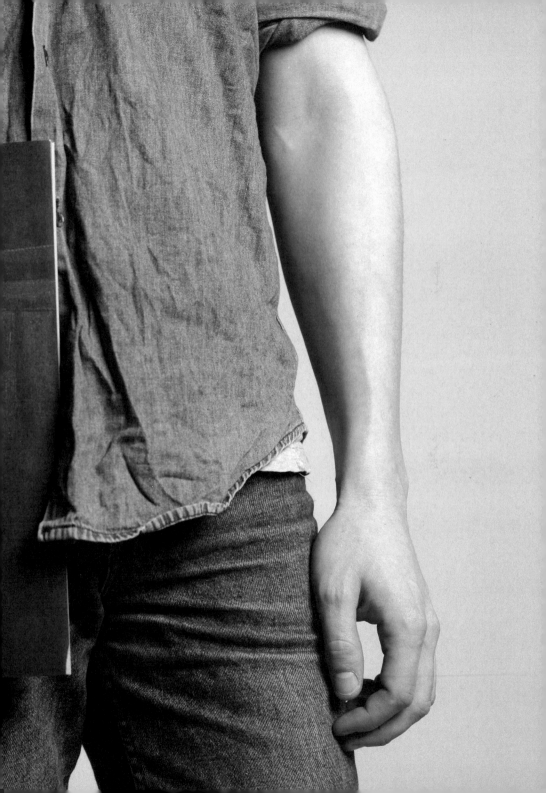

– *Any troubles?*

The Transference of Fashion

On Bruno's Interview Skills

David Ratmoko

There was some apprehension prior to the release of Sacha Baron Cohen's latest film, as he launched his third screen personality in *Bruno* (2008), his namesake, the fashion journalist and reporter for 'Austria gay-TV (OJRF).' Already in the run-up, writs were being issued alleging defamation of Austrians as 'Nazis in Lederhosen.'[1] Like his well-known alter-egos, Ali G. and Borat, Bruno comes from the controversial light entertainment programme, *Da Ali G Show* (2002–2004), the embryo of Cohen's later films.[2] Whilst the class action over 'Nazis in Lederhosen' might prove that 'there is no such thing as bad publicity,' it also sums up the central theme of Bruno:

what do 'fashion' and 'fascism' have in common?

Despite their unrelated etymology, the two terms *fashion* and *fascism* have become so similar that the resulting neologism, *fashism* is an accurate description of Bruno's journalistic achievement.

A sparkling example is the episode 'Fashion Police' in which Bruno plays the modish game 'In or Out' with Leon Hall, a fashion guru and television presenter. Here is an excerpt from the interview:

> *Bruno:* 'Charlize Theron, in or out of the balloon?'
> *Leon:* 'In, she's just won the Oscars.'
> *Bruno:* 'Ricky Martin, keep him in the ghetto or

train to Auschwitz?'
Leon: 'Keep him in the ghetto.'
Bruno: 'Burt Reynolds, keep him in the ghetto or
train to Auschwitz?'
Leon: 'Auschwitz.'
Bruno: 'Jack Black, candy or cancer?'
Leon: 'Cancer.'

This 'exclusionary practice' (Michel Foucault) is based on the familiar 'sixth sense of fashion' (Walter Benjamin), a subjective feeling or avant-garde knowledge of who is 'in' at any given moment. Sometimes the question is just whether somebody has won the Oscars or has vanished from the scene. It has undertones of the fascist desire to overthrow anything which is old-fashioned or outdated. What is so alarming is the readiness to frame 'in' or 'out' in the terminology used for the Nazi deportations.

Are such statements pure stupidity, neo-fascism, un-subtle provocation, or are they induced by Bruno's loaded questions? Putting the suspicion of fascism to one side, easy though it may be to corroborate, it is necessary to clar-ify how Bruno entices the fashion world out of its shell or stirs it from the latent state, which until now had suited it well. The issue of Bruno's methods is of primary importance.

Bruno's Routine

In order to gain access to the demimonde of international fashion, Bruno uses a microphone (of the fictional station OJRF) with a cameraman following behind him. Equipped

105

in this way he finds it particularly easy to reach the back-ground people, the stylists, young designers, PR people and boutique owners who, longing for media presence, want 'just 15 minutes of fame' (Andy Warhol). During the interviews attention is continually focused on the camera, just as if the fashion designers being interviewed were themselves seeking the limelight. The media self-presen-tation of fashion, its dissemination in the form of photos, film, and language reveals itself as a kind of 'Vanity Fair' at which the 'language of fashion' (Roland Barthes) is understood by all involved.

Also Bruno likes to flirt with the camera, to such an extent that he hardly allows his interviewee space and always appears concerned not to drop out of the picture. He is the ultimate fashionista, a victim of fashion bent on reprisal, excelling in his use of the language of fashion. This intention is brought out in Bruno's weird, emphatical-ly individualistic clothing: sporting a sleeveless fishnet T-shirt and tight-fitting Lederhosen worn with a Mohawk, he practically eclipses his interviewee even before it becomes clear that there is no point in their both wooing the camera.[3]

Bruno also contrives the flow of the conversation right down to the last detail. The staged interview parodies a proven MTV or Fashion TV dramatisation which seems professional to the interviewee, but is increasingly em-barrassing for the viewer. Bruno's routine is to start with a flattering introduction: the stylist is introduced as a 'make-over messiah', the PR agent as 'God of seating orders' and the boutique proprietor as 'trendsetter of stars'. This kind of exaggeration reduces the level of inhibition in his inter-locutors and leads them to underestimate Bruno's poten-tial for criticism. The unsuspecting person is eased through the interview as all their answers are positively reinforced and accompanied by comments like 'that's great', 'wow' or hysterical laughter. Seemingly intent on always getting the best out of them, Bruno teases the most surprising state-ments from his interviewees.

Let's Party *Zusammenmachen*!

Bruno speaks English with a feigned German accent, uses made up German words, interspersing them with au-thentic German. His aggressive artificial German, as for example '*Vassup*' or '*Ich* don't think so', may be incompre-hensible to the viewers, but what matters is that it is rec-ognisable as German. His interviewees magnanimously overlook his relapse into German, as if these slips of the tongue gave them the upper hand. Not only does Bruno milk the bonus of posing as a foreigner with a pseudo-German accent, he also exploits two prejudices against Germans: he excuses his directness while obviating any ironical inference.

Considered in the light of the tradition of English litera-ture and the comedy film, Bruno's Austro-German origins are not auspicious. Compatriots like Dr. Frankenstein from Mary Shelley's novel or Dr. Strangelove from Stanley

Kubrick's film, leave a trail of destruction behind them, and in this respect Bruno is their successor. Peter Sellers, in particular, with whom Sacha Baron Cohen is eagerly compared, seems to have been behind the creation of Bruno, in his role as Dr. Strangelove, consultant and ex-Nazi. Just as Dr. Strangelove's right arm involuntarily shoots up in a Hitler salute, Bruno's English similarly slips back into German whenever he gets excited, as in 'Let's party *zusammenmachen!*'

There is another analogy: Dr. Strangelove in the film manages to discover a latent form of fascism in the Central US Command; Bruno's alleged origins and his 'no holds barred' attitude to history reveal a latent fascism in the fashion scene.[4] 'People who don't come from New York have no individual style,' opines an anonymous designer at the New York Fashion Week 2004. 'Why don't you just put them on the train?', Bruno probes, 'off to the camp, never to be seen again?' 'I'd just love to do that,' agrees the designer.

Class Distinction

Immediately following the catwalk show staged by Michael and Hushi, two young designers at the New York Fashion Week 2004, Bruno questions Roger Padhilia, the show's Casting Director. 'Many of the Austrian style gurus think that Osama bin Laden is the best dressed man. Is that what you think, too?' 'Yes, he is cool. I don't know whether he's the best dressed man but he's certainly fashionable.' Undoubtedly, answers like this satisfy the demand for controversial 'statements' in an avant-garde, which is how the world of fashion likes to be depicted. This is the case at the Heatherette Show, again at the New York Fashion Week: 'It's about trailer trash, clothes from hillbillies, who just wear what there is,' explains Tiffany, the stylist. Bruno follows on with his 'sorry-about-my-English-ploy' and paraphrases, 'so it's about primitive, trashy people?' Tiffany: 'Yes, kind of.'

> *Bruno:* 'Are you hoping these white trash people
> will buy the clothes?'
> *Tiffany:* 'I don't think they can afford to.'
> *Bruno* (laughing): 'They're too poor! It's like in Austria when we
> take the clothes of the homeless and sell them in boutiques.'
> *Tiffany* (laughing): 'Like puts the prices up!'
> *Bruno:* 'The homeless can't afford them!'
> *Tiffany:* 'Exactly.'
> *Bruno:* 'That's the beauty of fashion.'
> *Tiffany:* 'Yeah.'

The aesthetics of this sort of fashion defies an established pattern which implies, according to Georg Simmel (1911), 'that the fashions of the upper stratum of society are never identical with those of the lower; in fact, they are abandoned by the former as soon as the latter prepares to appropriate them.'[5] Even so the *trailer trash* collection is still bound up in the class syndrome, as the prices exclude the *white trash,* whereas the affluent class hold so-called *trailer trash* theme parties, amongst themselves of course.

This dividing line is more subtle and less easily crossed. Eduard Fuchs already identified the reason: 'It must...be reiterated that the concern for segregating the classes is only one cause of the frequent variations in fashions, and that a second cause – the private-capitalist mode of production, which in the interest of its profit margin must continually multiply the possibilities of turnover – is of equal importance.'[6]

Following Jesus

Surely it's ridiculous that politicians or doctors enjoy greater respect in society than stylists, Bruno asks on the occasion of the New York Fashion Week 2004. 'Yes, of course it is,' replies an anonymous stylist.

> *Bruno:* 'After all, fashion saves
> more lives than doctors, doesn't it?'
> *Stylist:* 'Yes, quite right.'

The response made by another stylist to the following loaded question sounds equally glib and smug:

> *Bruno:* 'Could the Second World War have been avoided if
> people had been better dressed at the time?'
> *Stylist:* 'Yes, of course it could.'

What sounds like arrogance, wishful thinking, or crass misjudgement can sometimes be understood as such. As when Bruno asks the stylist, described as a 'makeover messiah,' what he would give the *other* Messiah, Jesus

Christ. 'A pair of torn jeans, an open shirt and he would be a male model straight away,' he answers after lengthy reflection and without a trace of irony. The stylist goes on: '"the pretty boy look" would suit him or the rough "biker-Hollywood look".' And: 'he would look great on the cover of *Vanity Fair*, say with long hair, ruffled by the wind machine, a sensuous expression and a romantic outfit.' Are these the figurations of Christ which are impinging on the contemporary world of fashion? As improbable as this may sound, Christ as Christian was once the principle hero in *Vanity Fair*, not the magazine, but the chapter bearing the same name in John Bunyan's bestseller *Pilgrim's Progress* (1678).

The fixed routine of Bruno's interviews involves a constant change of posture. They start to converse standing up, then sitting, and finish reclining. Although the imposed structure appears more inhibiting than funky, none of the interviewees protests. And it is when reclining that the interviews either plumb the definitive depths or rise to the heights of embarrassment. A request is made for a personal contribution to a charitable cause ('charity' derives from Latin *caritas*) out of Christian love:

> *Bruno:* 'Our show is supporting a charity about deaf or dead children, who knows, and I'd like to ask whether you can do something for them into the camera?'

Amer, 'the trendsetter of stars', raises his arms in an incomprehensible gesture after Bruno explains to him that the deaf children would not be able to hear his verbal message. This is followed by unbearable minutes of silence. 'That really makes a difference,' Bruno comments. The love of one's neighbour also becomes unbearable in the episode with Paul Wilmot, the 'God of seating plans.' He is asked to instruct the same deaf children in 'sexual responsibility and safe sex.' After some abortive, verbal attempts Wilmot eventually mimes a message. To signify 'no' he wags his finger for about a minute at the camera. Apparently, the Christian institution of *charity* registers with them so strongly that none of the participants is aware of the absurdity of the 'personal contributions.'

Doing Politics

Can fashion set political trends, perhaps even promote political awareness? 'Yes!' thinks Shail Upadhya, fashion designer at the New York Fashion Week 2004. His answer to Bruno's question as to the purpose of his latest collection shows Upadhya's political will: 'It is *post 9-11* clothing.' The fashion on show at the Fashion Week was still much too *September 10.* The designer said he would have left clothing like this in the cupboard. Instead of probing what had been said, Bruno goes along with it:

> *Bruno:* 'Why don't we put all the clothes from before 9-11 on a big pile, hire a few terrorists and blow it all up?'
> *Upadhya:* 'That's a great idea!'

Perhaps Bruno's greatest strength is letting others think they have found an ally in him, somebody who thinks as they do, and is not afraid to put his cards on the table. Probably that is why the designer complies with Bruno's request to 'show the camera a September 12th face.' Upadhya stares fixedly into the camera and thinks this is an 'inscrutable face.' 'Now a September 10th face,' demands Bruno, whereupon the designer assumes a happy expression. And again 'a September 13th face' and now again 'a September 14th face,' demands Bruno. Visibly unnerved, Upadhya still tries to find a facial expression without understanding its purpose, whilst its effect, as a political performance, ebbs away into a total absence of expression. That is how fashion shows its political face.

The Who's Who of Identity Fraud

Just next door they are preparing for Carolina Herrera's Spring and Summer Collection. 'We have a slight problem. We can't get to Carolina Herrera, the designer,' Bruno explains to a woman associated with the fashion show. 'Could you pass yourself off as her?'

Woman: 'Where are you from?'
Bruno (whispering in her ear): 'From Austria,
they really haven't got a clue there!'
Woman: 'Of course. Shall I speak about the collection?'
Bruno (in the camera): 'Well, I'm here with Carolina Herrera, the
designer of the crazy Show. Well, Carolina, how's it been?'

Woman as Carolina Herrera: 'It was wonderful. My vision this year was to combine casual with elegant, and it really was an eclectic mix, very dichotomous.'

The identity fraud is blown, firstly because the scene is not cut, and then because the real Carolina Herrera is interviewed shortly afterwards. Bruno successfully employs similar conversation openers with less well-known fashion designers and meets with no reluctance to play the imposter. Everybody is prepared to play a role for the sake of 15 minutes of fame. And surprisingly they do it to perfection, and on demand. Under the false assumption that the interview would be cut later, those interviewed gladly fulfil Bruno's expectations.

Just like Amer, a designer and boutique owner in Melrose Avenue, who is asked what it was like when Madonna came into the shop. 'She never did,' he says by way of correction. After Bruno explains to him that Madonna is the reason for the interview, Amer takes another run at the same question:

Amer: 'It was really amazing.'
Bruno: 'How many clothes did she buy?'
Amer: 'Fourteen.'
Bruno: 'Is this Madonna's favourite shop?'
Amer: 'Yes, it is.'

Bruno's Transference

Just like Borat, Bruno is not a character with whom the masses identify. Unlike other television presenters, he does not present a viable alternative to the elite world of fashion. His role as a comic actor is more to express the unconscious desire of the masses and to pay the price for the transgressions himself or else to pass it on to his interviewees. On each occasion, Bruno prompts his opponent to say things in front of a live camera which should not have escaped censorship, the secrecy of confession or psychoanalytical confidentiality.

Indeed Bruno establishes with his interviewees a relationship of transference or *Übertragung* akin to psychoanalysis. Old wishes are re-articulated in his presence, and transferred into the present, in the belief that individual censorship would be replaced by the camera's editing out. Whether they be fascist desires or false identity, avantgarde longings or fantasies about Christ, the transference into the present occurs in competition with Bruno, who embraces them all, and with a view to the camera or microphone, from which global broadcasting is expected. In this 'lose-lose' situation the expected gain eludes everybody: the aspiring fashion designer; Bruno, the character, who is designed to be an aggressive rival and loser; and also the fashion industry in its relationship with its consumers.

---

1   According to a report of November 2006, Sacha Baron Cohen was supposed to appear in court again. Edward D. Fagan, the American lawyer, intended to act once more by issuing the writ; he had already taken on the action on behalf of the inhabitants of the Romanian village, Glod, who had complained about having been

depicted as incestuous in Cohens film *Borat* (2006). 'The reason for the contravention: Cohen is supposed to be planning a defamation of Austria in *Bruno*. The intent to do so is sufficient in itself for legal action, according to a confidante of Fagan, the lawyer. As soon as the feelings of one single Austrian are seen to have been affronted, a writ can be issued. According to reports in the media the Austrians are said to have been maligned in *Bruno* as "Nazis in Lederhosen".' (www.firstnews.de, 29.11.2006)

2 All quotations are taken from the episodes 'Funky Zeit with Bruno' by Sacha Baron Cohen. *Da Ali G Show: the Complete First Season,* New York, HBO Video, 2003. *Da Ali G Show: the Complete Second Season,* New York, HBO Video, 2005. *Ali G in da USAiii,* New York, HBO Video, 2005.

3 Part of Bruno's role is to exhibit a homosexuality that he employs to obtain respect and access to a homophile fashion scene. It is characterised by the stereotypes of over-enthusiasm, affectation and a compulsion to self-presentation: the very qualities reflecting the international fashion scene, and qualities in which Bruno in fact outdoes the latter.

4 Cohen's dual strategy is similar to the one he employed in *Borat* (2006), where the backwardness of Kazakhstan is used to expose the hidden foundations of American society.

5 Georg Simmel, *Philosophische Kultur,* Leipzig 1911, p.32. Quotation from Walter Benjamin, *The Arcades Project,* translated by Howard Eiland and Kevin McLaughlin, Cambridge, MA: Belknap 1999, p.77.

6 Eduard Fuchs, *Illustrierte Sittengeschichte vom Mittelalter bis zur Gegenwart. Das buergerliche Zeitalter,* Munich 1926, pp.53–54. Quotation from Benjamin, *Arcades Project,* p.77.

Wasteful and Skinny, but Rich of Signs

Paris Hilton and Fashion

Daniela Janser

'As far as both
Paris Hilton and her work on
herself are concerned,
it is no longer possible to
differentiate wealth,
opaqueness and generosity
from capriciousness,
simple-mindedness and
a natural penchant
for coincidence – if this is
not critical art, then
such a thing never existed.'

Dietmar Dath

The Simple Life, Season 3, USA 2005
Video stills

In his *Theory of the Leisure Class* Thorstein Veblen wrote a slender chapter on the topic 'Dress as an Expression of the Pecuniary Culture.'[1] The book came out in 1899 and therefore his theories refer to the era before the turn of the twentieth century:

1. Clothing is a very visible sign of wealth; therefore, price and exclusivity are its most important features: it is eye-catching and lavish.

2. Such clothing must also clearly emphasise that the wearers are not engaged in any productive work: it is therefore clearly impractical. This applies particularly to women's wear. The corset typifies the sort of encumbrance which makes it impossible to work. Productive work is seen to be rather unbecoming for the leisure class.

3. Expensive leisure wear is worn for a season at the most, and is therefore always up to the minute; that means it is short-lived. Besides, generally speaking, it is thought to be frightful and is only described as beautiful because it happens to be 'in' and is expensive.

Paris Hilton, seen as *the* icon of this millennium's new leisure class, seems at first glance to confirm every aspect of these hundred year old theories with only minor deviations. The corset has been superseded by a rigorous leanness – the aim is to fit an American size 0 – which again is equally unhealthy and unsuitable for work. Hilton is also the ideal rich girl in the way Veblen intended, because her *original* fortune is inherited and has therefore been acquired without any effort on her part. The fact that Hilton often offends 'normal taste' and looks like a whore – and curses and swears like one – is something which ordinary people are happy to reinforce; at the same time they derive some gratification from it, even if this is tinged with class-based resentment.

However, these areas of similarity do not of course represent the whole truth. Paris Hilton makes it quite clear that Veblen's theories have to be taken a stage further in their dialectic. As far as she is concerned leisure is certainly not 'idle bliss' but 'hard work.' The product is nothing other than herself: having spent 24 hours working on herself, the 'Paris Hilton' creation emerges via intensive communication channels, claiming public and media attention. The 'Paris Hilton product' which is being constantly worked on in this way is that of a *professional socialite.* She can even be hired as such for parties, openings of clubs, or for the ball at the Vienna Opera.

In his article originally published in the *Frankfurter Allgemeine Zeitung* entitled 'Nude, toppling downstairs,' Dietmar Dath compares two highly professional heiresses from different centuries: Peggy Guggenheim (who could be said to represent Veblen's era) and Paris Hilton as 'Prototype of the "Fin de siecle 2.0 series."'[2] Guggenheim has gone down in history as an art collector and promoter of avant-garde art; Hilton constantly showcases herself as a work of art, or more accurately as an 'obscene installation' or as 'critical art' which constantly works on itself, as Dath writes.[3]

The reality soap, *The Simple Life* (2003 ff.) is the perfect window for this insight. It is the microcosm within the main drama entitled *Paris Hilton's Life of Leisure.* (This 'drama within a drama' even takes on a slightly Shakespearean nuance: Hilton's part-time friend Nicole Richie, who plays her sidekick in *Simple Life*, is generally known as 'bastard' – she is the adopted daughter and heiress of the soul star, Lionel Richie.) Just as Paris Hilton creates and presents herself daily as a super rich, obscene installation, two millionaire heiresses parody the 'simple life' in the very successful TV series.

What is the role of clothing in this interlocking drama? Paris Hilton plays, sells and hires herself out as a commodity which is always exclusively packaged, i.e. clothed. No item appears twice in public and certainly no item may be worn again in which another woman has been photographed. This is part of Hilton's self-imposed code of conduct, the only one to which she resolutely holds. Consequently, it is only fashion, which is exclusive and reliable within the endlessly volatile, self-perpetuating loops which entwine the leisure class, reality show and celebrity industry. The aspiration to achieve size 0 is not simply fashion's zero point. Fashion is rather to be seen as the sole sphere in the Hilton Universe, which constantly flags up a significant event and makes a distinctive statement. 'I have never been to China before. I had no idea what to expect. But I love Chinese fashion,' she commented briefly for the record on a visit to Shanghai, wearing a high-necked little red silk dress as a gesture to Chinese fashion.

It is not then surprising that the signals received from Hilton's fashion code are more complex than most of the statements which she otherwise makes. In the pilot film for the first run of the *Simple Life,* the two heroines go shopping for the last time in military clothing before boarding a flight to the furthest point of the American world to sample life on a farm. Having arrived there and been called upon to carry out 'ordinary gainful employment' for the first time in their lives, they once more wear military camouflage. The choice of clothing leads to speculation concerning the similar nature of the two activities: shopping is Hilton's equivalent to work. And clothes are the means by which she expresses herself intellectually – this is no longer a mere symbol of wealth and addiction to extravagance, as it was previously in Veblen's theory.

Hilton, who does not wear a dress twice and communicates in code via her fashion, however occasionally does not wear any (special) clothing – and yet she stands out. The first instance of this was her notorious sex video *One Night in Paris,* the publication of which was as a typical example of a purposefully choreographed mishap. There was a second occasion during her spell in prison, of which we have no photographs, apart from the posed contrived photos of the British artist, Alison Jackson. In her volume of photos *Confidential: What You See Is Not Real,* Jackson choreographs, alongside many other celebrities, a Hilton double behind bars wearing an orange prisoner's overall or posing naked under the shower.[4] The porn video and the invisible spell in jail are the two naked exceptions in the life of this clothes' horse which, loaded with millions sends out its signs.

1   Thorstein Veblen, *Theory of the Leisure Class,* New York: Dover Publication 1994, pp. 167–187.

2   Dietmar Dath, 'Nackte, eine Treppe herunterpurzelnd: Peggy Guggenheim, Paris Hilton,' *Heute keine Konferenz: Texte fuer die Zeitung,* Frankfurt/M.: Edition Suhrkamp 2007, p. 278.

3   Dath, p. 280.

4   Alison Jackson, *Confidential: What You See Is Not Real,* Hong Kong, Cologne: Taschen 2007.

Learning from Louis Vuitton

The Originality of Fakes

Aude Lehmann

'How true is it that you are what you wear?', asks Bruno in his TV show *Funkyzeit with Bruno.* Of course my reply would have been: 'absolutely.' But what does it mean? How do we react to clothing which defines what we are?

We probably like fashion because it enables us to set ourselves apart from others and feel exclusive. How delightful to strut around in the latest item which we have found somewhere, knowing for certain that nobody else will be wearing that particular garment. (It is even more certain that nobody will be wearing it in exactly the same combination.) For a brief moment it is fun to feel that you are an 'explorer' who has selected something quite specific from a whole host of suggestions. It is wonderful to be original, even if it is only for a split second.

It can be just as exciting to start by noting how other people come to terms with fashion and then to make a decision based on that. It does not matter what people wear; by their choice of clothing they are telling a story, and they all embody a specific, or even a vague 'persona.' These observations may be simplistic and superficial and it would be easy to criticise the inappropriateness of 'cataloguing' people in this manner. But it is fascinating to reflect on its superficiality. I just assume that everybody who is in anyway interested in fashion, or to be more precise, everybody who is not completely indifferent to the clothes they put on each morning, is deliberately setting out somehow to represent 'something' or 'somebody' in the way they dress. 'I will wear something classical today. Or should I give my red shoes an airing? Or maybe that rather too colourful silk scarf? Is it a day for gadding about in something a little more elegant than usual? What's stopping me wearing my dress? Or is it better to be casual in jeans?' It all amounts to the fact that we project ourselves in ways which are subject to sudden alteration, a deliberate change of direction. And if everybody else also knows that 'you are what you wear', then you can go about it quite wilfully. You can perform your role just like an actor, or take on an unfamiliar role which just happens to appeal.

This is how fashion begins to work like costume and can be trotted out like a quotation. You assume a persona, a part in a narrative which has implications beyond yourself. The more varied the people are who acquire a specific garment, accessory or 'style,' the more fascinating it is to pursue their narrative. The garments become more complex because the different wearers or the roles they perform imbue them with a plethora of new meanings. This means that the cross references and implications, to which the combination of these characters gives rise, assume a greater importance than the individual outfits themselves. Whenever an appropriate garment is chosen, it is no longer possible to move outside the narrative associated with it. But there are still numerous possibilities for diversification. Depending on how, where and when the item is worn, new and original links can be established with other wearers – just as a variety of dialogues are possible within a story.

There are many examples of this kind of larger complex story: jeans, tee-shirt, sneakers. It would be quite implausible to try to present oneself as the principle person wearing jeans. It is much more convincing to feel that you are unique wearing your personalised jeans. If everybody is sporting tight-fitting trousers perhaps it is again time to go in for baggy. Or why not turn up at the next wedding in blue jeans after your friends have been discussing their evening dresses for weeks?

The narrative is even more interesting if something comparable happens with a label, because unlike a particular cut, type of dress or material, the label alone, by virtue of its signature, is associated with a certain degree of exclusiveness. But when a logo is suddenly worn by a large number of people, it gives rise to a complex interplay of 'originality' and the feeling of 'being a part of it.' Within an extensive narrative a whole range of characters with individual backgrounds and lifestyles assume particular and significant roles.

This is what happened in recent years to LV. Accessories which previously defined a specific target group were suddenly seen everywhere. It was as if a huge stage accommodated everybody. The classical combo of affluent mother, daughter, granddaughter may have found LV a little boring, but they carried on buying the multi-format set in the new collection almost every year. After years of begging, the granddaughter's school friend was finally given a small handbag for Christmas, as a collective present from the members of her family, who had put their money together. 50 Cent who dressed at some expense from head to foot in the LV style was, however, reluctantly served by the retailer because he appeared a little pretentious. Occasionally, Pharrell teemed up a discrete LV cap with the easy skater shirts from his own collection. Depending on their pocket money, the whole gang of hip hop teenagers from the school next door indulged in accessories from the LV shop or bought from a dubious market stall at the fair. The 35 year old graphic-designer-artist-DJ would buy a limited edition cap; he would do this because he listened to rap but thought, having seen out the actual hip hop era, he could tell the difference between art and commerce. The young mother, her life split between her studio and looking after the kids, enjoyed treating herself to something 'special' when going out, and caught the same bug as the African American family – mother, father and two small sons – who liked to take a stroll in the leafy suburb on Sundays, all sporting an LV cap and/or bag. The AD-CD sales promotion team downed a whiskey sour after work, but feigned collective surprise when they discovered that everybody had the same budget. The successful artist, who considered herself very well dressed and never really breathed a word about fashion, thought long and hard about whether she should fall back on her mother's original '60s LV bag for that private viewing, or should she after all carry the fake LV bag with the Velcro fastener, which she bought on her last trip to Sri Lanka?

In the end it was impossible to discover who was quoting whom; what had been started by whom – how and why – and who was making fun of whom? Who was serious; who was tongue in cheek; who was wearing a genuine article and who owned a good or a bad, genuine fake? The answer is of no consequence because they were all playing an important and unique role by being part of the LV story. It is, for this reason, a wonderful story when it comes to illustrating that we are *not* what we wear. Otherwise, how would it be possible for such a diverse crowd of people suddenly all to wear the same thing?

Jewels and Photography
Aubry B. Jewelry

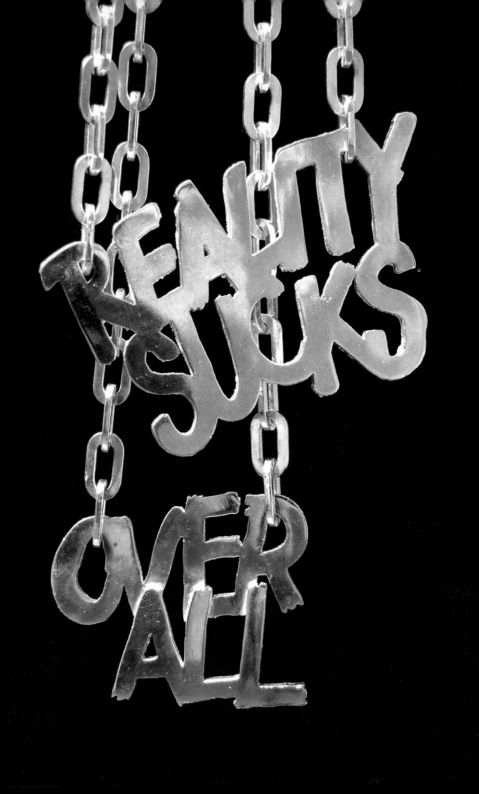

Ghetto Fabulous

Blackface Masquerade
from the Minstrel Show to Hip Hop

Susanne von Ledebur

Snoop (*1971) & Tupac (1971–1996)

Wiliams (1975–1922) & Walker (1873–1911)

Shortly after the premiere of his film *Bamboozled* (2000), Spike Lee, the director, met Tommy Hilfiger one morning whilst taking his daughter to school. 'Oh Spike, how could you do this?', Hilfiger whined, 'I've been giving money at the Martin Luther King fund and every summer I send ghetto black kids to camp.'[1] Hilfiger was complaining about the fictitious commercial which Spike Lee had incorporated in his film. 'Timmy, Timmy, Timmy', shout women in tight-fitting Hilfiger outfits. In the centre of the group is a man resembling Tommy Hilfiger supplying a host of advertising slogans: 'Just stay in the Ghetto! Stay broke!'

In this witty commercial Spike Lee was not only implying that Hilfiger and other (white) producers of hip hop outfits (such as Adidas a.o.) glorified ghetto and gangster life, but he was also associating them with the Minstrel Show. The commercial comes in the prelude to the *New Millenium Minstrel Show,* which is produced by the hero of the film, the African American TV producer Pierre Delacroix. Delacroix attempts to get himself sacked with his exceedingly stupid, racist programme about blacks, and in doing so pursues a strategy similar to the Jewish theatre producers in Mel Brook's famous Broadway play (and film) *The Producers.* They contrive to rip off the insurance company with what they suppose will be a certain flop: the antisemitic musical *Springtime for Hitler.* The joke however is, of course, that in each case the plays enjoy great success although, or rather *because* they are anti-semitic or racist.

In fact all the actors in Delacroix's show for the new millennium are black, but they appear, in common with the mainly white actors from the Minstrel Show of the nineteenth century, in blackface: with lampblack painted faces and exaggerated red mouths, a woolly wig and clownish tramp-like clothing. Such disguises which distort the appearance of African Americans in a grotesque and absurd manner emerged in 1820 in the north of the USA – mainly in New York – and enjoyed great popularity with an audience consisting of a predominantly white underclass. The black-faced characters were often poor, homeless, itinerant wretches who danced as they sang to the banjo about their misfortunes in an artificial black slang. One of the most famous was Jim Crow, invented and personified by the white actor, Thomas Dartmouth Rice. He was – at least in his early days – a heavy, ambiguous character: both victim and perpetrator, he did not take those in authority or himself seriously. In particular, he caused a stir by the way he danced; this was a variation on the dances which African Americans actually used to perform in the harbours of New York.

It was in the Minstrel Shows of the '40s that black-face scenes were expanded into whole evening performances and blackface characters became part of a set pattern. There was now an established range of characters starting with Jim Crow, followed by Bones and Tambo who were named after their instruments. They were extremely

50 Cent (*1975)

Sammie Russell (dates unknown)

musical but equally stupid, lazy and impudent (comparable perhaps to Harpo in the Marx Brothers). They stood out from the so-called interlocutor who appeared as master of ceremonies and spoke in eloquent, aristocratic English (a parallel with Groucho Marx). The Minstrel Show often began with a dialogue between the interlocutor, Tambo and Bones; the humour emerged from the two idiots' inability to understand the pretentious language. Other characters were Old Uncle and Old Auntie, two servants devoted to their slave-owner; also Dandy, an emancipated black townie who lived beyond his means, aping and parodying the language and manners of the upper class whites.

Numerous clownish, racist mascots, icons and brand names developed from these stereotypes in the course of the following decades. By the '50s most of these had disappeared when the Black Civil Rights Movement had become more influential. Amongst those still in existence today, 'Uncle Ben,' of the brand of rice with the same name, can be seen as a continuation of Old Uncle, and 'Aunt Jemima,' a brand of ready-to-eat pancakes widely distributed in the USA, is an offspring of Old Auntie. But the racist stereotype of the black who is uneducated, musical and always cheerful also arrived in cartoons. Walt Disney invented his Mickey Mouse as a character from the Minstrel Show in the late 1920s. With his white gloves Mickey not only looks like a blackface actor but in the early version he also dances and sings and is always ridiculously good-humoured.

The Minstrel Show was the first truly American theatrical form and was probably a model for various magnificent manifestations of contemporary stage performance. For example, the so-called *stump speech* – a monologue on any topic from politics, science to the latest gossip, which Bones or Tambo performed standing on a tree stump – is a clear forerunner of the stand-up comedians of today. For a long time the Minstrel Show was *the* way into show-business and fame for African American singers and actors. But since 1950 there has probably been no other branch of the performing arts which is so taboo. 'A comedy about slavery,' in Spike Lee's verdict, 'just about as amusing as a comedy about the Holocaust.'

It is not then surprising that Tommy Hilfiger was not happy when Lee presented a Tommy Hilfiger in the guise of a sponsor of the *New Millenium Minstrel Show.* It was a clear statement against the designer and also the hip hoppers who wear his clothing. For Spike Lee, as he made clear in a commentary, 'Gangsta Rap is nothing other than the twentieth century Minstrel Show.' Although Lee did not elaborate further on this point, one can easily leave it to the imagination. The Gangsta look or ghetto fabulous style – as P. Diddy called it – can be seen as a new mode of the Dandy figure from the Minstrel Show. In fact Spike Lee's analogy was not original. Stanley Crouch for one, the African American jazz critic, had repeatedly pointed out the parallels. He claimed that the Minstrel Shows owed their success to the fact that the racial stereotype was validated

Bert Williams (1975–1922)

Flavour Flav (*1959)

by the lazy, criminal black who stole such things as chickens and water melons, and he attributed the fame of contemporary rappers to the way they personified the alleged black lifestyle by their promiscuity and gangster existence.[2]

Similarly, W.T. Lhamon Jr., the American literary scholar, had shown that M.C. Hammer, in the video *Hammer Time* (1990), was performing the very same dance which was popular in the harbours of New York around 1820, and which T.D. Rice had adopted for his Jim Crow character.[3] However, Lhamon, unlike Lee or Crouch, had not made use of these parallels in order to denounce or criticise M.C. Hammer. On the contrary, in his study of early blackface performances, like Jim Crow for example, Lhamon discovered something other than racist overtones. To give one example, he shows that the blackface actors performed in areas inhabited by a mix of the black and white underclass, as in the seventh district of New York. In the 1820s African Americans used to dance there on the Catherine Fish Market in M.C. Hammer style; this was the same place in which one hundred years earlier the participants of an uprising had been executed in events recorded by history as the 'Negro Revolt,' although Spanish, Irish and English immigrants had been as much involved as African Americans.

Against this background Lhamon understands blackface as a cultural expression of a mixed ethnic underclass. In the early blackface performances he remarks the enormous fascination which the white actors had for 'black' gestures and modes of expression and he emphasises that the jokes were frequently not just applicable to the 'black' speaker but were equally directed at well-known authorities. The audience were not just laughing at the blackfaces but also identifying with them. It was an audience composed of young workers, Irish, French, German and English immigrants, and also African Americans who could identify with the misfortunes and social exclusion of somebody like Jim Crow, and later with Bone and Tambo. Consequently, before it became set into a crude stereotypical mould in the 1850s, blackface was part of the proletarian youth culture and exercised an attraction through its degree of street credibility. Characters like Jim Crow were so popular because they had, amongst other things, the aura of the outsider, the antagonist.

It is fitting then that the songs and jokes performed by the blackfaces often contained self-reflexive parts. In a famous number T.D. Rice, as Jim Crow, started by making fun of the whites with blackened faces who think that they can depict blacks; he then went on to lament the fact that *he* could not even go to see these dilettantes because blacks were not allowed into that particular theatre. Without denying that the blackfaces always had their racist implications, Lhamon manages on the basis of songs like this to bring out quite different facets and to depict what is on the whole a dazzling picture of the Minstrel Show.

Mos Def (*1973)

Eddie Cantor (1892 – 1964)

Spike Lee would then have been correct when he asserted that the current Gangsta Rappers are carrying on the blackface tradition; however, he is less justified in his assumption that this is merely an appropriation of racist iconography. In recent years the character of the pimp, who has become central in hip hop, can of course be seen as the perfect reincarnation of the racial prejudice which regards blacks as promiscuous and criminal. But do we really laugh at Snoop Dogg behaving like a pimp in his TV Show, *Doggy Fizzle Televizzle*? Or is it not obvious who the real procurer is by the time Snoop visits Hugh Hefner – and also who just skilfully mimics one?

Ultimately, Spike Lee knows how multi-faceted the blackface tradition is. In contrast to his detailed commentary on the film the short extracts from Delacroix's *New Minstrel Show* are at times extremely amusing. For the role of Sleep'n'Eat, one of the show's characters, Lee managed to hire Tommy Davidson, the well-known black comedian, and one of the numbers comes from his programme. In addition, Spike Lee relied directly on the tradition of the Minstrel Show for his own principle character: Pierre Delacroix, who speaks with an artificial English accent and with tremendous eloquence is clearly an imitation of the classical interlocutor. Thus, whilst Spike Lee emphasises in *Bamboozled* the racial tendencies of the Minstrel Show, his own film is itself such a show. In this way *Bamboozled* retains the quite brilliant ambivalence which was an aspect of the Minstrel Show and which still remains an important feature of the many contemporary performances of the Gangsta Rappers and the Hip Hoppers.

1   All Spike Lee quotes are taken from the 'Audio Commentary With Director Spike Lee' on the DVD release of *Bamboozled,* New Line Home Video, USA 2001.

2   Quoted in Jonathan Fischer, 'Ein Mann sieht schwarz: "Public Enemies", Flavor Flav und die Rückkehr rassistischer Klischees in den Pop,' *Sueddeutsche Zeitung,* 24.11.2007.

3   W.T. Lhamon Jr., *Raising Cain: Blackface Performance from Jim Crow to Hip Hop,* Cambridge, MA: Harvard UP 1998.

– Have you seen Toulouse?

Da Gucci, Da Fendi, Da Prada

50 Cent's More Than Conspicuous Consumption

Tan Waelchli

Since the emergence of Gangster Rappers, hip hop is seen as both more successful and worse than it ever was. Whilst Jay-Z, 50 Cent, P. Diddy, Snoop Dogg a.o. sell millions of albums worldwide, more demanding listeners complain about the commercialisation and the banality of the lyrics. People say things used to be better. Didn't hip hop arise as a subculture of a disadvantaged social group and advocate politically subversive views? On the occasion of the 2006 MTV Awards in New York 50 Cent gave a commentary on this view which was as apt as it was witty. When asked about his chances of winning a prize he roguishly replied,

'I usually don't get the awards I'm supposed to, but I always get my cheque.'

The fixation on money comes over particularly clearly when Jay-Z or Diddy describe themselves as 'entrepreneurs' building up commercial conglomerates which include disc labels, financial interests in film and television companies, their own lines of clothing and restaurants among other things. The almost mythical self-made men like Rockefeller who epitomise the 'American Dream' serve as their role models. The clothing and lifestyle of the Gangster Rappers is modelled on this social elite. They prefer to wear expensive suits – 'da Gucci, da Fendi, da Prada,' like 50 Cent boasted in his hit *P.I.M.P.* (2003) – and they spend vast sums of money on cars, yachts, villas and never-ending parties. However, the association with role models like Rockefeller is not entirely untarnished. When, for example, Jay-Z calls his clothing label 'Rock A Fella,' there is an unmistakable note of parody. And when Snoop produces porno videos or markets ordinary products like grill accessories, the image of the great entrepreneur is defaced.

The chasm which opens up here is greater than it sometimes appears at first glance. Although the Gangster Rappers claim to be American self-made entrepreneurs, they are far from being elevated into the social elite. They are not even accepted by the producers of luxury goods whose customers they are. For example, not a single Gangster Rapper has yet been offered this sort of advertising contract, and hip hoppers only very rarely feature in photo stories to be found in fashion magazines. It is also well known that Gucci is not best pleased when P. Diddy occupies the flagship store in Milan for hours on end with his crew. Although rarely mentioned in public, there is a real concern that these escapades could deter certain sections of the regular clientele, and there is an instance of such observations even leading to a blistering scandal. When in the summer of 2006 the CEO of Roederer, the champagne producer, was openly critical of the fact that the reputation of their superior brand 'Cristal' had been diminished by the excessive consumption of the hip hoppers, Jay-Z felt insulted, spoke of racism and removed the name of 'Cristal' from his lyrics and his bars.

However, it may well be doubtful whether the problem could just be solved with another brand of champagne, as Jay-Z thought it would. For the way in which the Gangster Rappers celebrate their glamorous lifestyle does not easily conform to the traditional image of superior products. The hip hoppers are just consuming 'too many good things' – whether they be clothes, alcohol, jewellery, cars or interior fittings. This is perceived by the upper classes to be in poor taste and commensurate with the Gangster Rappers' lack of education and 'culture.' They have never acquired a sense of style, nor have they learned how to cope with luxury goods. The question thus arises as to how they acquired their wealth. How was it possible to earn so much money without any education? How could it be done without the remotest appreciation of the true value of market products and any inkling of the fundamentals of capitalism? The clear, logical conclusion is that the way in which the rappers came by their gains was not all that it should have been.

It is this suspicion which forms the close link between the hip hop entrepreneurs and the gangsters. Are there not also clear signs of their mutual obsession with luxury goods? This at least is what Jim Sheridan shows in his biopic on 50 Cent, *Get Rich or Die Trying* (2005). In the film, depicting the youthful 50's drug-dealing career, luxury goods feature as the longed for unattainable status symbols of the ghetto kids. The young 50 invests his first fee in a pair of white sneakers which he sees in a shop window, and a few years later, thanks to the boom in crack, the long awaited dream of a white Mercedes S Class becomes a reality. 50 does not change his obsession with consumption when, shortly afterwards, having hit rock bottom, he is forced to pull out because of conflicts in the gang and takes up rap. Far from undergoing a conversion or climbing up the social ladder, he continues to live in the ghetto and remains addicted to a gangster lifestyle.

Seen in this context, the real reason for the rejection experienced by the Gangster Rappers is comprehensible. At issue is their lack of 'culture' and tasteless preoccupation with luxury goods, but essentially the problem is one of wealth not acquired 'in the correct manner.' It appears that the upper classes in this instance do not differentiate between drug dealers and hip hoppers – crack and break-beats are considered equally dangerous, and anybody selling them as consumer goods is ostracised by society.

On the other hand, the Gangster Rappers' immoderate preoccupation with clothes, champagne and cars etc. is to be seen as a performance. They demonstrate by their *flagrantly* 'tasteless' consumption that – given their occupations and their outlaw status – they will never belong to the ruling class, regardless of their wealth. They unmask the status symbols which set apart the social elite as reifications of illusory promises. Gangster hip hop thus reveals itself as a highly political movement; fashion and lifestyle are its essential means of political expression. By consuming 'too much of the good things' in an 'utterly tasteless' manner, the rappers reveal the false promise of the 'American Dream' of the self-made man, the dream of social advancement for all.

Automatisse

A La Mode

The Third Way of Fashion

Texte in Deutsch

„Oh la la, tu es à la mode!" – Die Formel, die auf Anhieb schmeichelhaft klingt, muss nicht immer als Kompliment gemeint sein. Obwohl Mode durchaus originell sein und eine geradezu avantgardistische Individualität zum Ausdruck bringen kann, verbindet man damit fast noch häufiger eine kommerzielle Industrie, die mit ihren zahllosen Kopien zur Uniformierung der Gesellschaft beiträgt. So verstanden bedeutet „modisch" sein gerade, *keinen* Stil zu haben und bloss mit der Zeit zu gehen. Und zu dieser Sichtweise scheint es passend, dass „être à la mode de quelqu'un", wie man den ganzen Satz rekonstruieren könnte, heisst, sich in der Art und Weise *von jemand anderem* kleiden. Und dies bedeutet immer eine Verfehlung. Man eifert einem modischen Vorbild nach, doch dabei lässt sich genau das nicht erreichen, was man sucht: die Originalität.

Vorbild und Nachahmung, Originalität und Verfehlung. In dieser Gegenüberstellung scheint die Alternative klar. Wer würde sich nicht auf die Seite der Individualität schlagen und die Industrie und den Kommerz ablehnen? Und doch: Besteht nicht das Paradox der Mode darin, dass sie, so „original" sie sich auch geben mag, immer schon nach Imitation verlangt? Arbeitet nicht die Mode – wie jede avantgardistische Bewegung – auf eine „kommende Gemeinschaft" hin, die eine Gemeinschaft des „Stils", des guten Geschmacks etc. wäre? So besehen macht es wenig Sinn, bloss die Industrie für die Massenprodukte verantwortlich zu machen, und den „originären" Gestus der Mode retten zu wollen.

Wie wäre es stattdessen, auf der Seite der Nachahmung zu beginnen; beim Bemühen, „à la mode" zu sein? Die Beiträge dieses Buches machen auf sich auf die Suche nach der modischen Verfehlung – im Film, in der Literatur, in Kunst, Mode, Fernsehen und in der Musik. Dabei zeigt sich, dass die Verfehlung nicht notwendig peinlich sein muss, und dass sie nicht immer zur Bestätigung des Originals und zur Uniformierung führt. Im Gegenteil: Unter Umständen kann „à la mode" zu einem eigenen Prinzip werden, zu einer neuartigen und gezielten Abweichung, die den Gegensatz von Original und Kopie aufhebt und eine dritte Position zwischen Avantgarde und kommerzieller Industrie ins Spiel bringt. „À la mode" zu sein heisst dann nicht mehr, „à la mode de quelqu'un", sondern „à la mode de n'importe qui".

Aude Lehmann & Tan Wälchli

176

Im Museumsshop
Die Mode als Schnittstelle von Kunst und Leben

Tan Wälchli

In den heutigen Museumsshops finden sich Objekte, die eine eigenartige Mischform von Kunst und Mode darstellen: Kleidungsstücke und Accessoires, die mit Abbildungen von Kunstwerken verziert sind. In den Guggenheim-Museen von Las Vegas bis Bilbao gibt es Pollock- und Kandinsky-Foulards zu kaufen, und im gemeinsamen Shop des Louvre und des Musée d'Orsay werden Krawatten mit Motiven von Monet oder Van Gogh angeboten. Während das touristische Massenpublikum an diesen Produkten offenbar Gefallen findet, gelten sie bei Kunst-Insidern als stillos; als Zeichen der unaufhaltsamen Kommerzialisierung und Banalisierung des Kunstbetriebs. Aber ist dieses Urteil nicht vorschnell und oberflächlich? Denn wenn die Übertragung der Kunst auf den Kommerz so reibungslos funktioniert, könnte dies nicht ein Zeichen dafür sein, dass die beiden Bereiche viel enger miteinander verwandt sind als wir meist annehmen mögen?

Zum Beispiel könnte man hier an Benjamins Beobachtung aus dem *Passagen-Werk* denken, dass die „Produkte" der Kunst sich seit dem Ende des 19. Jahrhunderts „als Ware auf den Markt […] begeben" hätten. Damit meinte Benjamin nicht etwa den Kunstmarkt, sondern er beobachtete, dass die künstlerischen „Gestaltungsformen" sich „von der Kunst emanzipiert" hatten und neuartige Gegenstände hervorbrachten, die als banale, kapitalistische „Waren" funktionierten. „Den Anfang machte die Architektur als Ingenieurskonstruktion.

Es folgte die Naturwiedergabe als Photographie. Die Phantasieschöpfung bereitet sich vor, als Werbegraphik praktisch zu werden. Die Dichtung unterwirft sich im Feuilleton der Montage."[1] Diese Entwicklung, so Benjamin, würde die Kunst nicht unbeschadet überstehen. Er bezeichnete die Kunstwerke als „Ruinen der Bourgeoisie", die durch die „Entwicklung der Produktivkräfte", welche die neuartigen Warenformen erzeugten, „in Trümmer gelegt" wurden.[2] Und in diesem Kontext von Photographie, Werbegraphik, Feuilleton etc. situierte Benjamin auch die Mode. Auch sie gehörte für ihn zu den neuartigen Waren, die durch die technische „Zertrümmerung" der bourgeoisen Kunsttradition entstanden.

Diese Bewertung lässt sich heute im Rückblick nachvollziehen. So betonte kürzlich die Kulturhistorikerin Nancy J. Troy, dass sich berühmte Pariser Modedesigner wie etwa Paul Poiret Anfang des 20. Jahrhunderts eng an der Kunst orientiert hatten. Wenn Poiret erklärte, er schaffe in seinem „Studio" mittels der Kleider ein „Porträt" seiner Kundinnen, erschienen seine neuartigen Waren als Transformationsprodukte der Porträtmalerei, und wenn er Kostüme für Theateraufführungen entwarf, die er nachher als Bestandteile seiner Kollektionen verkaufte, brachte er das Theater als „Ware auf den Markt". Dabei versuchte er anfänglich noch, seiner Kundschaft eine bourgeoise Exklusivität zu verkaufen, die er u. a. dadurch bewarb, dass seine Frau bei der Theaterpremiere im

Publikum als einzige bereits wie die Darstellenden auf der Bühne gekleidet war.[3] Bald jedoch machte sich auch in diesem Fall das von Benjamin beschriebene Problem bemerkbar, das die „Entwicklung der Produktivkräfte" bedeutete: Die grossen Warenhäuser in den USA begannen, Poirets Kreationen zu kopieren, und um die Raubkopien zu bekämpfen, blieb ihm nichts anderes übrig, als Lizenzverträge mit ausgewählten Warenhäusern abzuschliessen, denen er den Vertrieb seiner Modelle in Massenkollektionen gestattete.[4] In diesem Fall lässt sich also die Modeware, die es ab der Stange zu kaufen gab, exakt im Sinne Benjamins als ein „in Trümmer gelegtes" „Monument der Bourgeoisie" verstehen: Die Transformation der künstlerischen „Gestaltungsformen" in den Bereich der „Waren" – der Kleider – führte letztlich dazu, dass durch die „technische Reproduzierbarkeit" die Aura der Kunst „zertrümmert" wurde.

Besonders bemerkenswert an dieser Analyse ist, dass sie es auch erlaubt, die Innovation zu situieren, welche zur selben Zeit die verschiedenen modernistischen Bewegungen brachten. Sollte es ein Zufall sein, dass die Modernisten die tradierten künstlerischen „Gestaltungsformen" genau in dem Moment verwarfen, als sie „von der Kunst emanzipiert" worden waren? Jedenfalls prägten die Modernisten nicht nur völlig neue künstlerische Formen, sondern sie definierten auch das Verhältnis von Kunstwerk und Alltagsgegenstand in neuer Weise. Gemäss der Maxime „form follows function" sollten die alltäglichen Objekte nun gerade nicht mehr aus der Kunst abgeleitet werden, sondern in einer Weise, die ihrer „Profanität" angemessen war, möglichst nüchtern und praktisch gestaltet werden.

Dennoch aber wurden die beiden Sphären auch nicht getrennt, sondern die Verbindung wurde sogar noch intimer, wie sich daran ersehen lässt, dass viele Künstler auch im Bereich des Design tätig waren. Am treffendsten lässt sich der neuartige Bezug wohl mit Nietzsches Begriff des „Stils" beschreiben. Als „Mitteilung" einer „inneren Spannung von Pathos durch Zeichen" verstanden, steht der „Stil" bei Nietzsche für die alltägliche Äusserung einer neuartigen Kunsterfahrung, in der das Pathos zuerst erzeugt wird.[5] Dies heisst, dass die neuartige, „stilvolle" Gestaltung der Lebenswelt als eine *Folge* der neuartigen Kunst zu verstehen ist, die eine völlig neuartige Erfahrung von Pathos möglich gemacht hatte. Die Designobjekte, die sich von den Massenwaren – den „Trümmerstücken" der „bourgeoisen Ruinen" – radikal unterschieden, sind somit zugleich Ausdruck eines radikal anderen Kunstbegriffs.

Aus dem neuen Verständnis von Kunst und Stil ergab sich die avantgardistische – oder, in Nietzsches Begriff, „unzeitgemässe" – Haltung der Modernisten. Einerseits sollte die neuartige Kunsterfahrung allen zugänglich sein, und dem entsprach, dass die „stilvollen" Objekte, welche diese Erfahrung zum Ausdruck brachten, „technisch reproduziert" werden sollten. Andererseits aber befanden sich die Modernisten in einem dauernden Kampf mit dem noch nicht weit genug entwickelten Bewusstsein der Massen, die noch am bourgeoisen Kunstverständnis festhielten und sich an den daraus abgeleiteten kapitalistischen Waren vergnügten. Deshalb waren die

Modernisten zwar auf Massenwirksamkeit bedacht, aber zugleich auch höchst elitär, und dies äusserte sich darin, dass einerseits die Designobjekte nur in sehr kleinen Auflagen produziert wurden oder sogar Unikate, Prototypen, blieben, während andererseits Abbildungen davon in den Massenmedien in möglichst grossen Auflagen verbreitet werden sollten – um eben das Bewusstsein der Massen vorteilhaft zu beeinflussen.[6]

Blickt man von heute auf dieses Projekt zurück, so zeigt sich, dass es den Modernisten bisher nicht gelang, das Massenpublikum umzuerziehen. Noch immer ist der Design-Kult heute ein elitäres Phänomen. Aber noch immer, so scheint es, hält auch der Modernismus an seinem ursprünglichen Antrieb fest: Wer heute einen besonderen Zugang zur post-bourgeoisen Kunst zu haben meint, bringt dies nach wie vor durch die elitäre, stilvolle Gestaltung seiner Lebenswelt zum Ausdruck, und noch immer geht es dabei darum, in den Massenmedien abgebildet zu werden. Nicht zuletzt gilt dies für die heutige Designer-Mode, wie sich z.B. an glamourösen Veranstaltungen wie der Oscar-Verleihung zeigt. Hier tragen die Stars für einen einzigen Abend ein möglichst exklusives Stück eines bekannten Designers, um auf dem roten Teppich durch die Fotografie und das Fernsehen in massenmediale Bilder transformiert zu werden. Und ist die Logik des „prototypischen" Gegenstands nicht überhaupt der Antrieb der heutigen Modewelt? Wer etwas auf sich hält, wird ein bestimmtes Kleid niemals bei mehr als einem wichtigen Anlass tragen, und deshalb können Berühmtheiten wie Lady Di oder Madonna ihre Garderobe von Zeit zu Zeit versteigern lassen – wobei dann von jedem Kleid angegeben wird, wo und wann es getragen worden war. So lässt sich die

Designer-Mode als eine avantgardistische, künstlerische Gegenbewegung zu jenen industriell gefertigten Warenhaus-Kollektionen verstehen, welche die traditionelle, bourgeoise Kunst in „Trümmer" gelegt hatten.

1 Walter Benjamin, *Das Passagen-Werk, Gesammelte Schriften* V.I, Frankfurt/M.: Suhrkamp, 1982, S.59.

2 Benjamin, *Passagen-Werk*, S.59.

3 Vgl. Nancy J. Troy, *Couture Culture: A Study in Modern Art and Fashion*, Cambridge MA: The MIT Press, 2003, S.51,.209.

4 Vgl. Troy, *Couture Culture*, S.269.

5 Friedrich Nietzsche, „Ecce Homo", in: *Kritische Studienausgabe* VI, München: de Gruyter, 1999, S.304.

6 Vgl. dazu Beatriz Colomina, *Privacy and Publicity: Architecture as Mass Media*, Princeton: Princeton UP, 1993.

Warum trägt Roger Buergel rote Jeans?
Bemerkungen zur Ideologie der freien Wahl

Tirdad Zolghadr

Soso, Herr Direktor Buergel trägt rote Jeans. Und zwar eine Art helles Scharlachrot, wie man es aus deutschen Soziologie-Departementen und holländischen Provinz-Discos kennt. Gelegentlich trägt er auch schwarze Waffenrock-Hosen, und wenn er zum Rednerpult schreitet, zieht er den elastischen Gurt um die Hüfte hoch, so dass sich im Schritt ein hübscher kleiner, Hackey-Sack-artiger Bobbel bildet. „Sehr menschlich", wie die Deutschen sagen.

Jetzt denkt mal an Okwui zurück. Okwui Enwezor ist immer perfekt angezogen – Shirts von Richard James, Slipper von Gucci – und er spricht in theoretischen Piktogrammen und akademischen Metonymien. Locker entlarvt er Metadiskurse und wer auf einer Konferenz mit ihm zu diskutieren versucht, verstummt angesichts der Pirouetten, die er dreht, um zur nächsten Frage überzugehen. Im Vergleich dazu klingt Buergel, wenn er Enwezors Ausstellungen als „Zoos" denunziert und stattdessen „gemeinsame psychische Erfahrungen" fordert, wie ein Berliner Student, der mit Kuba-Solidaritäts-Aktivisten durchs Land tourt und Beedees rauchend am Lagerfeuer sitzt.

Beedees oder Davidoff. In einem historischen Lexikon las ich einst, dass Nikita Chruschtschow sich gelegentlich ein Partyspiel genehmigte, bei dem zu nächtlicher Stunde und nach vielen Runden Wodka Orange alle am Tisch mitmachen mussten. Das Spiel heisst *La question qui tue* und besteht darin, dass

man jemanden vor eine „unmögliche" Wahl stellt: Pelmeni oder Blini. Puschkin oder Dostojewski. Malerei oder Fotografie. Screwdriver oder Bloody Mary. Gucci oder Prada. Christian Boltanski oder Ilja Kabakow. Einige meiner Freunde fanden vor ein paar Jahren Gefallen daran, und seither hat sich das Spiel als todsicheres Mittel erwiesen, um bei nächststehenden Kollegen unerwartete Ideologien aufzuspüren, bei romantischen Paaren Zwietracht zu streuen und Dinner Partys in grundlose Polarisierungen ausarten zu lassen.

Das Verblüffende daran ist die allegorische Wucht, die eine Frage wie Britney oder Amy, Hillary oder Barack, Shahrzad oder Whyart zu entwickeln vermag. Sie lässt die Wahl zwischen Regen und Traufe spannend, anregend, ja sogar erfreulich erscheinen. Allein dadurch, dass das autonome Subjekt auf der Skala des Immergleichen die eine – und nicht etwa die andere! – Abstufung wählt, scheint die Annahme bestätigt zu werden, dass die zwei Vorschläge, aus denen die Frage einen Gegensatz konstruiert, effektiv in kolossaler Opposition zueinander stehen. Denn warum sonst sollte es nötig sein, zur Begründung der getroffenen „Wahl" auf die subtilsten rhetorischen Tricks zu verfallen?

Die erfundenen Kontraste zwischen grösstenteils deckungsgleichen Figuren lassen hervortreten, dass die freie Wahl ein ideologischer Apparat ist, der jene unzähligen Distinktions-Spiele antreibt, die nicht nur den Habitus von Kurato-

rinnen und Kuratoren prägen. In einer Zeit, in jede künstlerische Technik (ebenso wie jeder politische Stil und jedes Modestatement) taktisch missbraucht oder strategisch wiedererweckt werden kann, anstatt dass wir in Ruhe die geweihte Geschichte irgendeiner intellektuellen Tradition geniessen dürften, verlangen diese Spiele eine beträchtliche Kunstfertigkeit. Wie kann eine freie Wahl noch von Gewicht sein, wenn heute sowieso jeder Konsens erbittert unterlaufen wird – und zwar dank eines verblüffend breiten Konsenses darüber, dass wir uns, wenn es anders wäre, in eine Horde faschistischer Hyänen verwandeln würden?

Lässt man das Versprechen auf gute Unterhaltung, auf „Sound and Fury", mal beiseite, so hat die Ideologie der freien Wahl vor allem den Effekt, dass sie verbirgt, wie limitiert unser Freiraum tatsächlich ist: beeinflusst von Peergroups, persönlichen Eitelkeiten, Sprachbarrieren, EU Förderpolitik, Klassenherkunft, hartnäckigen ästhetischen Ideologien und Flugtarifen. Istanbul oder Berlin. Sharjah oder Singapur. Die reine Routine, mit der die „kreativen" Berufe heute betrieben werden, zwingt uns dazu, unsere Entscheidungen, selbst wenn es nur formelhafte Kompromisse sind, ins Dramatische zu überhöhen und dem Publikum als gefährliche Balanceakte auf einem radikalen dritten Weg zu verkaufen. „Ich sage NEIN zum Ästhetizismus und NEIN zum Dogma des Politaktivismus – *denn wir brauchen SOWOHL Ästhetik als auch Politik!!!*" Oder aber wir lehnen es wütend, eifrig, hartnäckig ab, eine Wahl zu treffen, und bevorzugen es, irgendwo entlang einer symmetrischen Mitte in einem kritischen Dilemma stecken zu bleiben: „Die Revolution ist tot und Liberalismus bedeutet Kompromisse. *Was also sollen wir tun!!!"* *Tristesse Royale* oder *No Pasaran*. So bleibt heute jede kritische Veranlagung entweder mit der traurigen Melancholie der „unmöglichen" Wahl verbunden, oder aber mit der ehrenhaften Verantwortung, die es mit sich bringt, die „richtige Wahl" getroffen zu haben. Das kommt dem ritterlichen Universum von Don Quichote näher als dem globalen Dorf, in dem wir angeblich leben.

Cross-dressing Class
Der Hochstapler als Travestiekünstler

Florian Keller

Der Daumen seiner rechten Hand steckt lässig in der Hosentasche seiner Jeans, mit der andern Hand kratzt er sich gedankenverloren am Kinn. Sein unschuldiger Blick geht zur Seite, schüchtern vielleicht oder ungläubig. Und über der Magengegend der rote Schriftzug des Labels: *Pepe Jeans, London*. Ein anderes Bild zeigt ihn ähnlich verträumt, aber in selbstbewusster Pose, mit nacktem Oberkörper jetzt, und über den Armen der rote Schriftzug des Labels: *Emporio Armani*. Schliesslich sehen wir ihn noch einmal, wiederum mit nacktem Oberkörper, aber sein Blick wirkt nun fordernd, direkt auf den Betrachter gerichtet. Über dem Oberarm ist ein Flacon abgebildet, darunter der weisse Schriftzug des Labels: *Gucci*. Und so sollte dieser schöne junge Mann, für ein paar Tage wenigstens, nationale Berühmtheit erlangen: als „Gucci-Schwindler".

Seine selbst gebastelte Gucci-Werbung drehte der 25-jährige Juan Isidro Casilla im Februar des Jahres 2007 einer Schweizer Gratiszeitung an, zwei Tage später brachte er es gar zu einer doppelseitigen Anzeige in der grossformatigen *SonntagsZeitung*. Als falsches Armani-Model hatte er sich zwei Monate zuvor schon einen Hochglanz-Auftritt in einem Schweizer Modemagazin verschafft, ohne dass jemand Verdacht geschöpft hätte. Nur das Schwulenheft, dem er noch früher seine Jeans-Werbung unterjubeln wollte, hatte dankend abgelehnt. Der wirtschaftliche Schaden, den die Casilla mit seinen gefälschten Anzeigen verursachte, wurde auf 100'000 Franken beziffert. Der theoretische Mehrwert, den er nebenbei erzeugte, lässt sich auf folgende These zuspitzen: Die Figur des Hochstaplers ist das perfekte Subjekt der Mode.

Als Wiederholungstäter macht der Hochstapler den Wunschtraum und das Versprechen der Mode wahr, wonach jedes neue Kleid, das wir tragen, uns zu dem macht, was wir sein wollen: „Erschaffe dich selbst! Erschaffe dich immer wieder neu!" Diesen autopoetischen Zauberspruch der Mode nimmt der Hochstapler beim Wort. Und wie die Mode braucht er das Scheinwerferlicht, um zu glänzen: Er spielt unter den Augen der Öffentlichkeit, denn im Zwielicht ist es ihm nicht hell genug.

Der Hochstapler ist nicht zwingend ein Betrüger. Er setzt sich immer über soziale Schranken hinweg, aber nicht unbedingt über das Gesetz. Schon in seinen Anfängen definiert er sich zuallererst über den Look, der mehr aus ihm macht, als er ist. Als der Begriff des Hochstaplers im 18. Jahrhundert erstmals auftaucht, bezeichnet man damit Bettler, die sich über ihren sozialen Status erheben, indem sie sich äusserlich mit dem Schein des Vornehmen bekleiden. Ein Begriff aus der *Queer Theory* drängt sich auf: Der Hochstapler ist ein *cross-dresser*, der sich auf der Bühne gesellschaftlicher Differenzen bewegt. Und seine Show hiesse demnach *Cross-dressing Class*. Es ist eine Travestie, die weniger mit Geschlechteridentität als mit den Kennzeichen sozialer Unterschiede spielt.

Den wohl grössten Virtuosen dieses Spiels hat Woody Allen in einem Film entworfen, der seinerseits als hochstaplerisches Kunststück angelegt ist. In seinem fingierten Dokumentarfilm *Zelig* (USA 1983) erfindet er einen Jedermann namens Leonard Zelig (gespielt von Woody Allen selbst), der als unauffälliger Mitläufer durch die Geschichte des 20. Jahrhunderts geistert und sich in einer stupenden Mimikry stets seinem jeweiligen sozialen Milieu anpasst. Unter

Gangstern wird Zelig zum Gangster, unter Rabbinern wird er zum Rabbiner, unter Nazis zum Nazi.

Als „menschliches Chamäleon" ist Zelig ein radikal modisches Phantom: Einerseits absolut konformistisch, zugleich aber immer wieder neu und deshalb nicht zu fassen, verkörpert er das fundamentale Paradox der Mode in einer Person. Aus diesem inneren Widerspruch ergibt sich auch die ironische Pointe, wenn Zelig sich zum Schluss des Films, von seinem pathologischen Anpassungsreflex geheilt, in Amerika zu einer individuellen Persönlichkeit ausbilden lässt. Indem er nach seiner Therapie geradezu modellhaft den amerikanischen Individualismus verkörpert, hat sich Zelig nämlich auch nur der herrschenden Lebenspraxis angepasst. Das ist die abgründige Tragik, die in Woody Allens Film nachwirkt: Der geheilte Zelig bleibt auch dann ein Chamäleon, als er endlich wie ein guter Amerikaner gelernt hat, für seine Haltung einzustehen und zu sagen, was er denkt.

Vom Nobody, der sich als Model ausgibt, über den Bettler, der sich als Edelmann aufführt, bis hin zum menschlichen Chamäleon namens Zelig: Als cross-dresser unterhöhlen die Hochstapler die Codes, welche die Zugehörigkeit zu einer sozialen Gruppe regeln. Wie sehr es dabei konkret auch um Dresscodes geht, zeigt Steven Spielbergs Film *Catch Me if You Can* (USA 2002), der die Eskapaden eines realen Hochstaplers und Scheckbetrügers nachzeichnet. Leonardo Di Caprio spielt Frank William Abagnale Jr., der Ende der 60er-Jahre die öffentliche Fantasie dermassen beflügelte, dass man ihn für seine Abenteuer als falscher Pilot bald auf den Kosenamen „James Bond der Lüfte" taufte. Schon als Schuljunge beschafft er sich ohne jegliche Ausbildung die Uniform eines Pilo-

ten der Pan American Airways – und von dem Augenblick an, da er sich mit dem symbolischen Stoff bekleidet, *ist* er ein Pilot, weil man ihn als solchen anerkennt.

Als Dienstanzug bildet die Uniform in gewisser Weise das Gegenstück zum individualistischen Versprechen der Mode. In der Disco oder auf dem Laufsteg mag die Uniform eines Piloten als nonkonformistisches Fashion-Statement wahrgenommen werden, im Flugverkehr hingegen ist sie Arbeitskleidung nach Vorschrift. Wenn sich der Held in *Catch Me if You Can* dadurch eigenmächtig zum Piloten befördert, ist das gleichwohl ein Beleg dafür, dass er als Hochstapler das grundlegende Paradox der Mode zwischen Avantgarde und Massenkultur verinnerlicht hat. Die Uniform nämlich weist ihn einerseits als blossen Nachahmungstäter aus, der dem mondänen Bild des Piloten nacheifert; andererseits ist es gerade diese Uniform, die es ihm ermöglicht, auf radikal individuelle Weise – ohne die Legitimation, die er als Pilot nötig hätte – das Versprechen der Mode von einer glanzvollen Selbstschöpfung wahr zu machen. Umgekehrt aber heisst dies, dass seine Extravaganz immer schon angepasst ist. Er lebt von der paradoxen Fähigkeit, ein herausragender Anpasser zu sein. Und genau im Moment, als sein Talent erkannt wird, wird er religiert zu dem, was er wirklich ist: ein Blender, der über seinen Verhältnissen lebt.

Spielbergs Film ist nun vor allem deshalb interessant, weil er – wie es bei Woody Allen bereits angedeutet ist – den Hochstapler als pragmatischen Vollstrecker des amerikanischen Traumes vorführt. Als im Elternhaus das bürgerliche Familienglück zerbricht, weil ein Steuerstreit den Vater in den Ruin treibt, verschafft sich der Sohn die ausgleichende Gerechtigkeit für

diesen sozialen Niedergang, indem er den Traum vom Erfolg stellvertretend für seinen Vater erfüllt: Mit falschen Schecks bringt er es zu materiellem Wohlstand, als falscher Arzt, Pilot und Rechtsanwalt stattet er sich mit dem symbolischen Kapital der High Society aus. Damit setzt der jugendliche Held in *Catch Me if You Can* jene Fiktion für sich in die Tat um, die der amerikanische Traum aufrecht erhalten soll: den Mythos nämlich, der die unbegrenzte soziale Mobilität behauptet.

In Amerika ist die Klassengesellschaft zwar nicht aufgehoben, aber vorgeblich so durchlässig wie nirgendwo sonst auf der Welt. Der Weg zum Erfolg und zum gesellschaftlichen Aufstieg, so will es die Verfassung, steht allen gleichermassen offen. Dieses Versprechen lässt sich, wie der Held in Spielbergs Film zeigt, leicht als Einladung zur Hochstapelei verstehen. Der Hochstapler arbeitet darauf hin, soziale Schranken spielend zu überwinden – von nichts Anderem handelt auch der amerikanische Traum. Oder weiter zugespitzt: Der amerikanische Traum ist eine kollektive Fantasie, die das Selbstverständnis des Hochstaplers in ein demokratisches Erfolgsversprechen verwandelt.

Der Titelheld in F. Scott Fitzgeralds *The Great Gatsby* (1925) ist ein schillerndes Beispiel dafür, und sein tragisches Ende erinnert an die dunkle Kehrseite dieser Fantasie. Wer sich wie Jay Gatsby auf das amerikanische Versprechen vom „guten Leben" beruft, vertraut in seinem Streben nach Glück darauf, dass man seine Vergangenheit jederzeit hinter sich lassen und sich neu erfinden kann. *You can find happiness by being someone else*, so die bestechende Formel, die der Kulturkritiker Frank Rich für den amerikanischen Traum geprägt hat. Das ist die Maxime des Hochstaplers, umgewertet zu einem nationalen Erfolgsmythos.

Vielleicht ist es deshalb kein Zufall, dass der grösste literarische Amerika-Erfinder auf europäischem Boden ein vorbestrafter Hochstapler namens Karl May war, der sich als Schriftsteller mit den biografischen Daten seines erfundenen Old Shatterhand schmücken sollte. Für

die fotografische Beglaubigung sorgte Karl May eigenhändig, indem er sich in der vollen Montur des Westernhelden ablichten liess – der Schriftsteller als Dressman seiner literarischen Fantasien.

„I'm nothing, really", sagt der Held in *Catch Me if You Can* einmal

von sich. Das ist der beklemmende Verdacht, von dem uns die Mode und der amerikanische Traum erlösen wollen. Aber nur der Hochstapler sieht die unerschöpflichen Möglichkeiten, die sich aus dieser traurigen Selbsterkenntnis eröffnen: *I'm nothing, really. Let's dress up!*

Don't Mock the Clothes!
Der modische Existentialismus von „Sex and the City"

Simone Meier

Es war einmal die schönste Fernseh-Serie der Welt. Die mit den schönsten Kleidern, aber auch vielen schönen Menschen, schönen Locations und irrsinnig schönen Dialogen. Frech, sexy, schnell und stylish. Es war die Glam-Rock-Version einer Serie. Sie hiess *Sex and the City*, handelte von vier heterosexuellen Single-Frauen namens Carrie, Samantha, Charlotte und Miranda in New York, die ganz und gar von Homosexuellen zurecht design worden waren. Vom schwulen Darren Star geschrieben und von der lesbischen Patricia Field ausgestattet. Und beinah restlos alle Frauen auf der Welt fanden sich irgendwo darin wieder.

Die Subkultur hatte den liebsten Zauberspiegel des Mainstreams erfunden und darin einen Traum platziert, den plötzlich alle leben wollten. Den Traum der emanzipierten, beruflich erfolgreichen, sexuell aktiven, finanziell unabhängigen und überaus attraktiven urbanen Single-Frau, die ihre Existenz dermassen im Griff hat, dass nicht nur sie selbst, sondern ihr ganzes Leben als Träger von begehrenswerten, überholten oder einfach nur unbeschwert

schönen Fashion-Items oder Accessoires verstanden werden kann. Mode als Metapher für das moderne Mädchendasein. Und Mode als Zugpferd für eine weltweit erfolgreiche Serie. Mode als Indikator einer gehobenen Globalität. Der Globalität der Luxuslabels nämlich, die sich zumindest die Protagonistin von *Sex and the City*, die blonde Beziehungskolumnistin Carrie Bradshaw, im Leben nie hätte leisten können, hätte es sich bei der Serie um eine realistische Abbildung der berufstätigen New Yorkerin gehandelt.

Aber um Realismus ging es nicht. Es ging vielmehr um die Darstellung realer Begehrlichkeiten, die sich in der Serie wieder und wieder märchengleich erfüllen durften. Die Frage war nicht mehr: Findet die Frau ihren Prinzen? Sondern: Findet die Frau ihr männliches Accessoire, aber gelingt es ihr vorher noch so schnell wie möglich aus eigenen Mitteln die neue Fendi-Handtasche oder die neuen Manolo Blahniks zu ergattern? Und da sich jede Frau auf der Welt unter Prada, Dolce, Chanel, Dior, Fendi etwas vorstellen konnte, weil es in jeder

grossen Stadt der Welt die betreffenden Läden schon längst gab, viel länger als die mächtigen Gleichmacher H&M oder Ikea und oft auch schon viel länger als das Internet, weil diese Label bereits Globalisierungsgewinner waren, bevor man von der Globalisierung überhaupt zu sprechen anfing, verstand auch jede Frau auf der Welt *Sex and the City*. Ein Vergleich wie „Clooney is like a Chanel suit. He'll always be in style" (Samantha) oder „My marriage is a fake Fendi" (Charlotte) leuchtet überall sofort ein. Und nichts ist griffiger als „A relationship is like couture. If it doesn't fit perfectly, it's a disaster" (Samantha).

Sorgen ob der globalisierten Uniformität macht sich in diesem Segment überraschenderweise niemand. Erklären lässt sich dies am besten mit Ermenegildo Zegna, dem italienischen Herren-Luxuslabel, das jahrelang mit Adrien Brody warb und sich im Winter 2007 mit dem Slogan „great minds think alike" profilierte. Grosse Geister denken ähnlich. Und ziehen deshalb das gleiche an. Man kann gar nicht anders. Die exklusive Uniformität ist chic und jedes entsprechende Kleidungsstück auch automatisch ein essentielles Stück Persönlichkeit, das mit einer grossen emotionalen Bindung getragen wird. „Don't mock the clothes", mach dich nicht über die Kleider lustig, weist Carrie einen unverständigen Lover zurecht. „Swear on Chanel", fordert sie vom gleichen Mann, als er versprechen muss, ein Geheimnis für sich zu behalten. Menschen sind fehlbar. Mode nicht. Ein Kleid ist, was es ist: In jeder Hinsicht schön und vollkommen, sonst nichts. Man könnte dies als die unbeschwerte Laufsteg-Variante des Existenzialismus bezeichnen.

Die Sprache (mit) der Mode bedeutet in *Sex and the City* auch eine Verdinglichung und Entsentimentalisierung der weiblichen Welt, ohne diese ihrer ästhetischen Eigenschaften zu berauben. Manchmal funktioniert das sogar fast ohne Label-Dropping. „A squirrel is just a rat with a cuter outfit. City girls are just country girls with cuter outfits", folgert Carrie nach einem

unglücklichen Besuch auf dem Land. Auf Samanthas sich auf sehr wenige Episoden beschränkendes Geständnis „I'm a lesbian" antwortet die rothaarige Miranda: „I forgot to tell you: I'm a fire hydrant", und Schuhfetischistin Carrie sagt das Naheliegendste: „I am a shoe." Woraus Samantha dann aber der Fassbarkeit halber doch folgern muss, dass sexuelle Orientierung nichts sei als „a label, like Gucci or Versace".

Höhepunkt des modischen Existenzialismus in der Serie ist Carries Teilnahme an einer Modeschau. *The Real Me* heisst die Episode, und auf dem Laufsteg, flankiert von prominenten Amateur-Models wie dem *New York Times*-Kolumnisten Frank Rich und der echten Heidi Klum, findet Carrie in einer glitzrigen Unterhose von Dolce & Gabbana ihr wahres Ich. Ein selbstbewusstes, gestärktes, glamouröses, selbstironisches Siegerinnen-Ich, das nach einem peinlichen Sturz auf dem Catwalk wieder aufsteht und alle

mit ihrer Performance übertrumpft. Ein stolzes Bild weiblicher Selbstermächtigung. Und wie fast alle *Sex and The City*-Kostüme dürfte auch die glitzrige Unterhose ihren zweiten Frühling in der Vintage-Boutique von Patricia Field in Manhattan erlebt haben. Field nämlich wurde mit dem Verkauf der einmal von den Schauspielerinnen getragenen Luxusfähnchen steinreich.

Einzig im Angesicht der Schöpfung selbst wird die Mode in ihre Schranken verwiesen. Wenige Folgen nach Carries Laufsteg-Triumph nämlich benetzt der gebärende Hydrant Miranda Carries bisher teuerste, mit rosa Tüll verzierte Aschenbrödel-Schuhe mit Fruchtwasser: „And thus, with a destroyed pair of Christian Louboutins, began Miranda's delivery", hören wir Carrie aus dem Off. Und freuen uns, dass selbst etwas so Grundprofanes wie eine geplatzte Fruchtblase seither mit einem hochkarätigen Label verbunden werden kann.

Viktor & Rolf, ich liebe euch (fast)

Cynthia Leung

Lieber du

Das hast du voll versaut, nicht? Sollte ich grosszügiger sein und sagen, dass *wir* es versaut haben? Ich will schreien, ICH HASSE DICH, doch sofort schütze ich mich mit der Vision eines Viktor & Rolf-Kleids: einer bauschenden Robe, auf der I LOVE YOU steht, ein Triumph der Schamlosigkeit über die Trauer.

Es war spontan und fühlte sich gut an. Ich fragte dich um deine Hand: Sollen wir? Willst du? Du sagtest ja. An einem Strand in Hong

Kong nach der Hochzeit eines Freundes. Es hätte nicht postkartenromantischer sein können – wie klischiert von mir. Ich trug ein weisses, zugeknöpftes Kleid von Helmut Lang und fühlte mich unverschämt. Vierzig Jahre später werde ich vermutlich sagen, dass ich nie mehr schöner aussah.

Du sagtest, dass du einen Tag früher daran gedacht hattest, mir dieselbe Frage zu stellen, als wir im Dunkel durch den Dschungel gewandert waren. Wir hatten es aufgegeben, meinen Lieblingsstrand zu

erreichen, weil die Sonne unterging. Also kehrten wir zur Zivilisation zurück. Ich erinnere mich an den Rückweg beim Schein unserer Handys, die Schatten erzeugten eine romantische Angst. Wie damenhaft von mir, im Dunkeln deine Hand fester zu fassen, als kleines Zeichen von Verletzlichkeit!

Egal. Nach Sophias Hochzeit nahm ich die Sache in meine eigenen Hände, und du sagtest ja. Was störte es, dass wir *high* waren? Am nächsten Morgen bedauerte ich nichts. Du auch nicht (sagtest du).

Von da an war es eine kleine Serie von Ankündigungen, unter Freunden und in der Familie. Wir flogen nach Spanien und kundschafteten eine vergoldete Kirche aus, einen bärtigen Priester sowie einen kleinen Leuchtturm an der östlichsten Spitze des Landes, dort, wo Salvador Dali und Gala ihr verrücktes Liebesnest gebaut hatten. Dem britischen Besitzer des Leuchtturms schrieben wir einen Brief: Ob er so freundlich wäre, uns den Turm für unser Hochzeits-Fest zu vermieten? Als er lachend erklärte, „alle Leute denken, dass ihre Liebe speziell ist", und nach mehr Geld fragte, dachten wir, was für ein Trottel, aber insgeheim brachten wir ab diesem Moment die Bremsen in Stellung.

Wie hätte ich besser über die Panne hinweggehen können als damit, mich auf das Kleid zu konzentrieren? Heimlich war das für mich eine wichtige Frage. Ich bin keine Prinzessin, ich hatte nie über meine Hochzeit oder über mein Hochzeitskleid fantasiert – aber nun war dies eine Herausforderung: mir ein Kostüm vorzustellen, das die Ewigkeit-in-einem-Tag verkörpert. Mich im ultimativen Symbol unserer Liebe zu kleiden, um der gefühllosen Welt – und dem britischen Leuchtturm-Trottel – zu beweisen, dass ich die Liebe gegenüber dem Hass bevorzuge.

Ich habe diese Fantasie nie mit dir geteilt. Es war mir peinlich, zuzugeben, dass sie existierte. Aber du bist eitel, also musst du es hören. Jetzt kommt alles raus, so wie deine kleine schmutzige Wäsche, die sich unerwartet mit meiner vermischt hatte.

Es gab mehrere Kandidaten. Zum Beispiel ein Hochzeitskleid von 1940, das ich vor Jahren in einem kalifornischen Second-Hand-Laden gekauft hatte, weil es ein Schnäppchen war. Vielleicht könnte ich es auf eBay verkaufen, dachte ich, an eine blonde Dame, die ihre Freude hätte an dem glänzenden Satin, den gepufften Ärmeln, den kleinen Knöpfen und der aufwändigen Spitzen-Schleppe. Vielleicht würde es eine ältere Braut sein, die sich auf ihren zweiten Gang zum Altar freute und bereit wäre, in die Vergangenheit einzutauchen? So hättest du mich nicht so sehen wollen, und ich auch nicht.

Dann tauchte als neue Vision Elsa Schiaparelli's Hummer-Kleid auf, ein schlaues, angemessen surrealistisches Statement für die Gelegenheit, für die surrealistische Sache der Hochzeit. Für einen Tag wäre ich der Hummer am Meer, in Spanien. Rot, bereit zum Fang, mit hässlichen Klauen und dem ganzen Rest. Schnell fand ich jedoch heraus, dass das Kleid ausser Reichweite war, da ich weder eine mächtige Kuratorin am Metropolitan noch eine entfernte Verwandte von Schiaparelli bin. Das Hummer-Kleid lebt nur in der Vitrine.

Dies war der Moment, als ich an Viktor & Rolf dachte. Vergiss die Geschichte, sagte ich mir, was ich brauche sind fantastische Designer und ein paar Dollars, um mir den Luxus leisten zu können. Und dies wurde zum Bestandteil unserer Streitereien. Eine kleine Träne. Vielleicht hab ich tatsächlich mehr für Designer-Schuhe als für Abendessen mit dir ausgegeben.

Später, als du darauf beharrtest, dass auch ich in unserer Beziehung gelogen hatte, erwähntest du den Tag, an dem ich aus dem Bett geschossen war und erklärt hatte, ich ginge früh arbeiten, morgens um Sieben. Stattdessen stand ich um halb Acht in der Schlange vor dem H&M in Soho, erpicht darauf, Viktor & Rolfs Kollektion für die Massen zu sehen. Ich gebe zu, dass ich neugierig war auf die ironischen Hochzeitskleider, die beim Eingang hingen.

Inmitten des Tumults schien das falsch, wie eine Blitzheirat in einem Vorort von Las Vegas: eine traurige Behauptung, dass man sich à la Britney Spears aus der Affäre jederzeit zurückziehen könne. Stattdessen brachte ich einen Smoking nach Hause, und still bemerktest du sofort meine kleine weisse Lüge. *Liar, Liar, pants on fire.*

Die Sache wurde komisch. Und schliesslich erinnerte ich mich an Viktor & Rolfs Witz einer Robe, ein Hochzeitskleid für eine Drag Queen. Dieses absurde Stück könnte passen. Es ist zwar eher ein Szenario als ein Kleid: als hätte ein kicherndes Mädchen mit roter Kreide „I Love You" auf das Bettlaken gekritzelt, um es sich dann wie eine Toga umzuwickeln. Nur zum Spass, um Erwachsensein zu spielen, für niemand bestimmtes. Das wäre ein unbändiges „Fuck You" an die Adresse des Leuchtturm-Besitzers gewesen, oder vielmehr, wie ich jetzt sagen würde, die weisse Flagge. Der letzte Atemzug … siehst du denn nicht? ICH LIEBE DICH.

Ich stellte mir vor, wie es wäre, das Kleid anzuprobieren, sein Inneres zu erkunden. Ich fühlte das Gewicht der dicken Schichten von königlichem Seiden-Satin, den kurzen Moment von Platzangst, wenn ich nicht herausfinden würde, wie man reinkommt, wo der rechte Arm hingehört, wo der linke; wenn ich mit geschlossenen Augen den Kopf ducken würde. Ich fühlte meinen zaghaften Versuch, nach Luft zu schnappen, die Spannung im Magen und die Prozedur des Ausziehens, um die unausweichliche Ausflucht zu nehmen.

Ich setzte mich sogar mit dem richtigen Viktor und dem richtigen Rolf in die Lounge eines deprimierenden amerikanischen Warenhauses, wo ich vernahm, dass das Kleid, das ich in meiner Fantasie getragen hatte, Celine Dion gehört! Vermutlich hängt es unberührt in Celine's Schrank in Las Vegas. Spiel mir das Titellied von *Titanic*, bitte!

Wie ich dich kenne wirst du mein pathetisches Gerede über das richtige Kleid für unelegant halten. Was gibt es in unserer Beziehung noch zu beweisen, ausser, ihre Leiche zu exhumieren? Mir scheint aber, ich kann mich noch immer da hinein versetzen, um dir eine Serie von verwirrenden Tunnels, falschen Sicherheits-Taschen und aufgegangenen Nähten zu zeigen. Und Schichten um Schichten von Tüll, die eine Oberfläche stützten, welche langsam in sich zusammensank und schliesslich kollabierte. Du konntest das auch fühlen, nicht? Oder hattest du dir vorgenommen, einfach einen Smoking zu mieten?

Wo immer du bist. Ich bin froh, dass wir es nicht geschafft haben. Ich bin glücklich, dass *ich* zuerst *dich* gefragt hatte. Ich denke nicht mehr über unser Scheitern nach, aber manchmal denke ich an das ungeheuerliche Viktor & Rolf-Kleid, dem der Körper fehlt, welcher dem I LOVE YOU Gestalt geben könnte. Es ist nur ein schwebendes Gespenst, ein leeres Versprechen, das ich in Gedanken anprobiert habe. Es gehörte mir nie, und umso einfacher ist es, es gehen zu lassen. Ich … vergebe dir.

Tschüss,
Miss C. Havisham

Die Doppelform
Plädoyer für das Model

Anus Belkrem

Als bekannter Friseur mit einem grossen Kundenkreis im Fashion-, Film- und Kunstbereich werde ich häufig zu Vernissagen eingeladen. Ich gehe fast immer hin, schliesslich muss ich in Kontakt bleiben, aber meist befällt mich beim Betrachten der Werke eine gewisse Ratlosigkeit. Es hat damit zu tun, dass das Kunstwerk nicht unbedingt gut aussehen muss und man einem Kunstwerk deshalb nicht mehr ansehen kann, ob es gut oder schlecht ist. Das Entscheidende, was die Qualität eines Kunstwerks ausmacht, scheint im Verborgenen zu liegen. Man sieht zwar die Form, aber den Inhalt sieht man nicht.

Um den Inhalt zu verstehen, sind die meisten Leute auf Hilfe von aussen angewiesen, z.B. auf die Hilfe der Spezialisten, die in Kunstkatalogen die Texte schreiben. Sie scheinen zu wissen, was es ist, das da im Verborgenen liegt, und sie können das Werk deuten. Aber ich lese solche Texte nie. Sie erinnern mich an die „Making-of"-Beiträge über Filme. Da kann ich mir auch nie vorstellen, dass sich das jemand anschauen mag. Es ist doch, wie wenn ein ernst zu nehmende Mode-seiner Vorstellung seine Tricks verrät. Und so ist auch es mit dem Inhalt und dem Kunstwerk.

In der Mode ist es einfacher. Mode hat keine tiefere Bedeutung, sie muss nur gut aussehen. Es gibt keine ernst zu nehmende Modetheorie und dafür kann man dankbar sein. In der Mode ist das Kleid die Form und die Person, die es trägt, ist der Inhalt. Deshalb sieht man hier im Gegensatz zur Kunst beides, die Form und den Inhalt. Die Person, die im Kleid steckt, ist in erster Linie das Fotomodel, welches das Kleid präsentiert. Der Auswahl eines Fotomodels wird grösste Aufmerksamkeit geschenkt, was richtig ist, denn schliesslich geht es um den Inhalt. Aber hier macht sich ein neues Problem bemerkbar: In der Regel sucht man bei einem Fotomodel nach einer möglichst idealen Form. (Zwar gab es schon viele Experimente, bei denen man Kleinwüchsige, Behinderte oder Alte über den Laufsteg schickte, aber wie man unschwer sehen kann, funktioniert das nicht.) Und dieses Streben nach der guten Form, für die es klare Definitionen gibt (Länge zu Höhe zu Breite etc.) bewirkt, dass der Inhalt unbestimmt wird.

Vielleicht müsste man deshalb sogar sagen, dass die Mode ganz ohne Inhalt auskommt. Denn das, was auf den ersten Blick als Inhalt erscheint, das Model, folgt ebenfalls ganz und gar dem Prinzip der guten Form, so dass eine Art Doppelform zustande kommt. Und da das Fotomodel tatsächlich nichts anders kann, als gut aussehen (wenn es singen, schauspielern oder tanzen könnte, würde es eben singen, schauspielern oder tanzen) wird es schwierig, der Mode überhaupt zu einem Inhalt zu verhelfen.

Ehrlich gesagt, mir ist es lieber, wenn etwas keinen Inhalt hat, als wenn der Inhalt verborgen ist.

The Kate Show
Die Ikone zwischen Porträt und Model

Aude Lehmann & Tan Wälchli

Im Herbst 2006 kuratierte Olivier Zahm im Amsterdamer Fotografie-museum (foam) eine Ausstellung über Kate Moss, *The Kate Show.* Gezeigt wurden neben Arbeiten von Mode-Fotografinnen und Foto-grafen – Jürgen Teller, Inez van Lamsweerde, Terry Richardson u.a. – auch Werke von Künstlern, die sich mit Kate beschäftigt hatten, z.B. Richard Prince und Andro Wekua. Erschien das Supermodel somit als eine Figur, die in der Kunst eben-so zu Hause ist wie in der Mode, sprach Zahm in diesem Zusammen-hang von einer „Ikone". Ihn interes-siere „die Tragödie, die die Pro-duktion der Ikone bedeutet, sowohl für die Leute, die sich von ihr dis-tanzieren als auch für jene, die in ihrem Licht leben."[1]

Was hat es mit dieser Definition auf sich? Wenn Zahm die Ikone sowohl in der Kunst als auch in der Mode situiert, dann lässt sich das so verstehen, dass sie einen Schnittpunkt der beiden Bereiche bildet. Und dies könnte daran erin-nern, dass Kunst und Mode im Normalfall getrennt sind: Das Kunst-werk ist original, während das Mode-bild in den Magazinen und auf den Plakaten technisch reproduziert wird. Auch inhaltlich gibt es eine gewichtige Differenz: Obwohl Kunst- und Modebilder häufig ähnlich aussehen, besonders im Bereich des Porträts, zeigen die Bilder nicht dasselbe: In der Kunst stehen die Menschen im Vordergrund, in der Mode hingegen die Kleider.

Künstlerische Porträts folgen bestimmten Bildkonventionen. Die Leute werden in typischen Settings gezeigt, mit repräsentativen Kleidern und Statussymbolen ausgestattet und in bestimmten Posen inszeniert. Dies bewirkt, dass die dargestell-ten Personen einem gewissen Ide-al angenähert werden, und unter Umständen wird man dabei sogar versuchen, die Gesichtszüge zu idealisieren. Aber bei all dem gilt, dass die Besonderheiten der einzel-nen Menschen letztlich erhalten bleiben: Spuren des Alters, des Be-rufs, gewisse Charakteristika des Gesichts oder ein bestimmter Blick. Dadurch entsteht eine Spannung zwischen dem konventionellen Bild und der abgebildeten Person. Die Besonderheit wird niemals ganz im Ideal aufgehoben – nicht einmal in der Aktmalerei, denn auch hier machen sich immer wieder körper-liche Besonderheiten – spezielle Proportionen, auffällige Falten etc. – bemerkbar.

In der Mode hingegen sind die Kleider das zentrale Sujet. Es han-delt sich um Prototypen, die einer noch nicht bestimmten Kundschaft angeboten werden. Diese Allge-meinheit verkörpert das Model. Es stellt ein gewissermassen virtuelles Ideal dar, und deshalb müssen die persönlichen Besonderheiten un-berücksichtigt bleiben. Zudem muss das Model – entsprechend den je-weils getragenen Kleidern – in ver-schiedene Rollen schlüpfen können. Sein Kennzeichen ist die perfekte Wandelbarkeit, wobei es jedoch stets dasselbe bleibt: das Model.

Der Gegensatz lässt sich ver-deutlichen, wenn man zwei Extreme vergleicht. Ein Künstler wie Lucian Freud schenkt in seinen Porträts den Besonderheiten der Menschen so viel Aufmerksamkeit, dass wir nur noch die Einzelnen mit ihren „Fehlern" sehen und das dahinter stehende Ideal fast vergessen. Hin-gegen rückt ein Modefotograf wie Helmut Newton das virtuelle Ideal manchmal derart deutlich in den Vordergrund, dass die Models all ihre Menschlichkeit zu verlieren drohen und beinahe wie Schaufens-terpuppen aussehen.

Wie lässt sich, wenn man von dieser Unterscheidung zwischen Kunst und Mode ausgeht, nun jener Schnittpunkt definieren, an dem sich die Ikone Kate befindet? Kate wurde Anfang der 90er-Jahre zu einer Zeit berühmt, als in Magazi-nen wie *ID, The Face* u.a. eine neue Art der Modefotografie entwi-ckelt wurde. Die Bilder sollten we-niger puppenhaft aussehen als bis-her, alltäglicher, und manchmal ging man sogar so weit, gewöhn-liche Leute von der Strasse in ihren eigenen Kleidern zu fotografieren. In diesem Umfeld konnte Kate – u.a. dank Fotos von Corinne Day oder Jürgen Teller – zu einer Reprä-sentantin des neuen Stils aufstei-gen, denn sie sieht für ein Model sehr speziell aus. Sie ist z.B. kleiner als im Normalfall verlangt wird – aber sie hat das „gewisse etwas".

Mit ihrem „nicht ganz" idealen, „irgendwie besonderen" Gesicht wurde Kate so berühmt, dass sie sich auch nicht mehr in eine Puppe verwandelte, nachdem sie – be-sonders dank den Werbungen für Calvin Klein Underwear – zu einem viel gebuchten Model für herkömm-liche Modefotografie geworden war.

Egal wie modellhaft sie inszeniert wird, wir erkennen Kate immer wieder, sogar auf einem Bild von Helmut Newton.

Deshalb gehört Kate niemals ganz zum Bereich der Mode. Zwar verkörpert sie, wie die anderen Models auch, das virtuelle Ideal, aber dabei schafft sie es irgendwie, nicht gesichtslos, puppenhaft zu werden, sondern – wie es sonst nur in der Kunst geschieht – ihre persönliche Besonderheit zu behalten. Anders als in der Kunst jedoch erscheint die Besonderheit des Menschen Kate nicht als „fehlerhafte" Abweichung von einem dahinter liegenden Ideal. Vielmehr scheint Kate paradoxerweise *in ihrer Besonderheit* das Ideal zu verkörpern. Sie bleibt zwar ein einzelner Mensch, aber *als solcher* stellt sie zugleich das virtuelle „Modell" der Modefotografie dar.

Nimmt man diese paradoxe Identität von Besonderem und Ideal als eine Definition der Ikone, erinnert dies an die alte Bedeutung des Begriffs. Ikonen waren ursprünglich jene Heiligen, die durch ihr vorbildliches Leben den gleichen Status wie Christus erreicht hatten: „Abbild Gottes" zu sein. Auch hier ging es also darum, dass ein virtuelles Ideal von einzelnen Menschen mit ihrem jeweils persönlichen Gesicht verkörpert wurde. Und dabei macht sich eine der verblüffende Folge der paradoxen Identität bemerkbar: Es zeigt sich, dass ein zur Ikone gewordener Mensch „hinter" seinem Bild nicht mehr existiert. Der Mensch, der das ideale „Abbild Gottes" verkörpert, *ist* dadurch zum Bild geworden.

Auch dieses Problem, so scheint es, stellt sich noch für eine heutige Ikone wie Kate. Es zeigt sich im

Fall der Paparazzi-Fotografien. Die Paparazzi versuchen, Kate als gewöhnlichen Menschen „hinter" den „virtuellen" Bildern zu zeigen, weshalb sie sich besonders für Skandale interessieren, in denen zum Ausdruck kommen, dass sie auch nur ein Mensch mit ihren Fehlern ist. Aber diese Attacke auf das vermeintlich „falsche" Bild des Models gelingt nicht. Selbst wenn wir Kate beim Kokain-Schnupfen sehen, schaffen wir es nicht mehr, in ihr etwas anderes als die Ikone zu erkennen, die wir in den Modemagazinen lieben gelernt haben. Kate bleibt Kate, egal ob in der Kunst, in der Mode oder auf den Fotos der Paparazzi.

1 „Das Magazin ist die Mode", in: Christoph Doswald (Hg.), *Double-Face*, Zürich: JRP|Ringier 2006, S. 88.

Die Übertragung der Mode
Zu Brunos Interview-Technik

David Ratmoko

Das Unbehagen war gross, als der neueste Film des britischen Starkomikers Sacha Baron Cohen erwartet wurde, der mit *Bruno* (2009) seine dritte Leinwandfigur ins Leben rief, nämlichen den gleichnamigen Modejournalisten und Reporter für „Austria gay-TV (OJRF)". Bereits im Vorfeld trafen Klagen ein wegen angeblicher Diffamierung von Österreichern als „Lederhosen tragenden Nazis".[1] Wie seine bekannten Alter-Egos Ali G und Borat entstammt auch Bruno der kontroversen Unterhaltungssendung *Da Ali G Show* (2002–2004), der Keim-

zelle von Cohens späteren Filmen.[2] Nach dem Motto „es gibt keine schlechte Presse" ist mit der Sammelklage über die „Lederhosen tragenden Nazis" sogleich das zentrale Thema von *Bruno* getroffen, nämlich die Frage, was *fashion* und *fascism* gemeinsam haben. Trotz unterschiedlicher Etymologien haben sich die beiden Begriffe *fashion* und *fascism* so angeglichen, dass die entstehende Neubildung *fashism* exakt Brunos journalistische Leistung bezeichnet.

Als schillerndes Beispiel steht die Episode *Fashion Polizei,* in der

Bruno das modische „*In oder Out*" spielt, und zwar mit Leon Hall, einem Fashion-Guru und Fernsehmoderator. Hier ein Ausschnitt aus dem Interview:

Bruno: „Charlize Theron, ist sie *in oder out*?"
Leon: *„In,* sie hat soeben den Oscar gewonnen."
Bruno: „Ricky Martin, im Ghetto lassen oder auf den Zug nach Auschwitz?"
Leon: „Im Ghetto lassen."
Bruno: „Burt Reynolds, im Ghetto lassen oder auf den Zug nach Auschwitz?"

189

Leon: „Auschwitz."
Bruno: „Jack Black, geben wir ihm *candy* oder *cancer*?"
Leon: *„Cancer."*
Grundlage für den „Ausschlussmechanismus" (Michel Foucault) ist die bekannte „Witterung der Mode" (Walter Benjamin), ein subjektives Empfinden oder Avantgarde-Wissen darüber, wer zurzeit angesagt ist. Manchmal ist die Frage bloss, ob jemand den Oscar gewonnen hat oder aber in der Versenkung verschwunden ist. Dahinter verbirgt sich der faschistische Wunsch, das Altmodische, sprich Überkommene, zu überwinden. Erschreckend ist die unverhohlene Bereitschaft, das modische *„In* oder *Out"* in den Begriffen der Nazi-Deportationen zu fassen.

Sind solche Aussagen reine Dummheit, Neo-Faschismus, misslungene Provokation oder provoziert durch Brunos Suggestivfragen? Den leicht zu erhärtenden Faschismus-Verdacht einmal beiseite, gilt es klarzustellen, wie Bruno die Modewelt aus der Reserve lockt, sprich, aus einer Latenz erweckt, die ihr bis anhin gut gestanden hat. Die Frage nach Brunos Methoden soll im Vordergrund stehen.

Brunos Routine

Um Zugang zur Halbwelt der internationalen Mode zu erlangen, bedient sich Bruno eines Mikrofons (des fiktiven Senders OJRF) und einer Kamera im Rücken. Besonders leicht gelangt er so an die Figuren im Hintergrund, an die Stylisten, Jungdesigner, PR-Leute und Boutiquen-Inhaber, die nach Medienpräsenz sich sehnend auch mal „für 15 Minuten berühmt sein" (Andy Warhol) wollen. Während der Interviews gilt die Aufmerksamkeit stets der Kamera, so als suchten die befragten Modemacher selbst das Rampenlicht. Die mediale Selbstdarstellung der Mode, ihre fotogra-

fische, filmische und sprachliche Verbreitung, entpuppt sich als ein „Jahrmarkt der Eitelkeiten", auf dem die „Sprache der Mode" (Roland Barthes) von allen Beteiligten verstanden wird.

Auch Bruno flirtet gern mit der Kamera, so sehr, dass er seinen Gesprächspartnern kaum Platz macht und stets besorgt erscheint, aus dem Bild zu fallen. Er ist der ultimative Fashionista, ein Modeopfer auf Rachezug, das die Sprache der Mode am besten spricht. Diese Absicht verfolgt auch Brunos schrille, die Individualität betonende Kleidung: ein ärmelloses Netz-T-Shirt, enge Lederhosen, getragen zu einem Irokesenschnitt. Damit stellt er seine Gesprächspartner gleichsam in den Schatten, noch bevor diesen klar wird, dass es sinnlos ist, mit ihm um die Kamera zu buhlen.[3]

Zudem bestimmt Bruno den Gesprächsablauf bis ins Letzte. Für die Inszenierung der Interviews parodiert er eine bewährte MTV- oder Fashion-TV-Dramaturgie, die auf seine Gesprächspartner professionell, auf den Zuschauer aber zunehmend peinlich wirkt. Routinemässig beginnt er mit einer schmeichelhaften Vorstellung: der Stylist wird als „make-over messiah", der PR-Agent als „God of seating orders" und der Boutiquen-Inhabers als „trendsetter of stars" vorgestellt. Solche Übertreibungen senken die Hemmschwelle des Gegenübers und verleiten dazu, Brunos Kritikvermögen zu unterschätzen. Um die Nichtsahnenden zur Fortsetzung der Interviews zu bewegen, werden alle Antworten positiv aufgewertet und von Kommentaren wie „das ist grossartig", „wow" oder hysterischem Lachen begleitet. Scheinbar stets bemüht, das Beste aus ihnen rauszuholen, entlockt Bruno seinen Gesprächspartnern die erstaunlichsten Aussagen.

Let's party zusammenmachen!

Bruno spricht Englisch mit einem gespielten deutschen Akzent, benutzt erfundene deutsche Wörter, lässt aber auch echtes Deutsch einfliessen. Sein aggressives Kunstdeutsch, wie *„Vassup"* oder „Ich *don't think so"*, mag den Gesprächspartnern und Zuschauern unverständlich sein, wichtig ist nur, dass die Sprache als Deutsch erkennbar wird. Seine Gesprächspartner schauen grosszügig über diese Rückfälle ins Deutsche hinweg, so als gäben diese Versprecher ihnen die Oberhand. Nicht nur kostet Bruno seinen Ausländerbonus voll aus, mit seinem gespielten deutschen Akzent nutzt er auch zwei kulturelle Vorurteile: er entschuldigt seine Direktheit und lässt keinerlei Ironie vermuten.

In der Tradition der englischen Literatur und Filmkömodie betrachtet, verheisst Brunos deutsch-österreichische Herkunft nichts Gutes. Landsleute wie Dr. Frankenstein aus Mary Shelleys Roman und Dr. Strangelove aus Kubricks gleichnamigen Film hinterlassen eine Spur der Zerstörung, in deren Nachfolge Bruno zu stehen kommt. Besonders Peter Sellers, mit dem Sacha Baron Cohen gerne verglichen wird, scheint als Dr. Strangelove, Berater und Ex-Nazi, bei der Schöpfung von Bruno Pate gestanden zu haben. So wie Dr. Strangeloves rechter Arm unwillkürlich zum Hitlergruss empor schnellt, wenn immer er sich erregt, so fällt auch Brunos Englisch unwillkürlich ins Deutsche zurück, wenn immer er sich begeistert: *„Let's party* zusammenmachen!"

Und ähnlich wie es Dr. Strangelove im Film gelingt, während des Kalten Krieges einen latenten Faschismus in der US-Kommandozentrale zu entdecken, so entdeckt Brunos vermeintliche Herkunft und tabuloser Umgang mit Geschichte einen latenten Faschismus in der Modeszene.[4] „Leute, die nicht aus New York sind, haben einfach keinen persönlichen Stil", meint eine ungenannte Designerin an der New York Fashion Week 2004. „Warum setzt ihr diese nicht einfach in den Zug", hakt Bruno nach, „ab ins Lager und auf nimmer Wiedersehen?" „Das würde ich liebend gerne tun", stimmt die Designerin zu.

Klassengrenzen

Unmittelbar nach der Laufsteg-Show von Michael & Hushi, zwei Jungdesignern an der New York Fashion Week 2004, befragt Bruno Roger Padhilia, den Casting Director der Show. „Viele der österreichischen Stil-Gurus meinen, dass Osama bin Laden der am besten angezogene Mann sei, meinst Du nicht auch?" „Ja, er ist cool. Ich weiss nicht, ob er der best angezogene Mann ist, aber bestimmt sehr modisch." Solche Antworten erfüllen zweifellos die Nachfrage nach kontroversen „Statements" in einer Avantgarde, zu der die Modewelt gerne stilisiert wird. So auch auf der Show von Heatherette, noch immer an der New York Fashion Week. „Es geht um *trailer trash*, um Kleider von Hinterwäldlern, die einfach anziehen, was gerade da ist", erklärt die Stylstin Tiffany. Bruno hakt mit seiner „Sorry-about-my-English-Masche" nach und paraphrasiert, es handle sich also um *„primitive, trashy people",* nicht? Tiffany: „Ja, in der Art."
  Bruno: „Hoffen Sie also, dass diese *white trash* Leute die Kleider kaufen werden?"
  Tiffany: „Ich glaube nicht, dass sie es sich leisten können."
  Bruno *(lachend)*: „Sie sind zu arm! Es ist wie in Österreich, wir nehmen die Kleider von Obdachlosen und verkaufen sie in Boutiquen."
  Tiffany *(lachend)*: „Setzt einfach die Preise rauf!"
  Bruno: „Die Obdachlosen können sie sich nicht leisten!"
  Tiffany: „Genau."
  Bruno: „Das ist das Schöne an der Mode."
  Tiffany: „Yeah."
Die Ästhetik dieser Mode durchbricht ein Muster, welches nach Georg Simmel (1911) besagt, „dass die Moden der höheren Schicht sich von der tieferen unterscheiden und in dem Augenblick verlassen werden, in dem diese letztere sie sich anzueignen beginnt".[5] Dennoch bleibt die *trailer trash* Kollektion im Klassenmuster verhaftet, da die Preise den *white trash* ausgrenzen, während die kaufkräftige Klasse sogenannte *trailer trash* Themenparties feiert, selbstverständlich unter sich. Diese Grenze ist subtiler und undurchlässiger. Ihren Grund erkannte bereits Eduard Fuchs: „Es muss […] wiederholt werden, dass die Interessen der Klassenscheidung nur die eine Ursache des häufigen Modewechsels sind, und dass die zweite: der häufige Modewechsel als Konsequenz der privatkapitalistischen Produktionsweise, die im Interesse ihrer Gewinnrate ständig ihre Absatzmöglichkeiten steigern muss, schliesslich […] ebensosehr ins Gewicht fällt".[6]

In der Nachfolge Jesu

Ob es nicht lächerlich sei, dass Politiker oder Ärzte ein höheres Ansehen in der Gesellschaft hätten als Stylisten, fragt Bruno anlässlich der New York Fashion Week 2004. „Ja, ganz genau", erwidert ein ungenannter Stylist.
  Bruno: „Denn die Mode rettet doch mehr Leben als die Ärzte."
  Stylist: „Ja, genau."
Ebenso unbegründet und selbstgefällig klingt die Aussage eines anderen Stylisten, der auf eine weitere Suggestivfrage Brunos wie folgt antwortet:
  Bruno: „Hätte der zweite Weltkrieg verhindert werden können, wenn damals die Leute besser angezogen gewesen wären?"
  Stylist: „Ja, bestimmt."
Was nach Überheblichkeit, Wunschdenken oder eklatanter Fehleinschätzung klingt, kann manchmal nachvollzogen werden. So fragt Bruno den als „make-over messiah" bezeichneten Stylisten, Daniel Dicrisio, welches *make-over* er dem *anderen* Messias, Jesus Christus, verpassen würde. „Ein paar zerrissene Jeans, offenes Hemd und er wäre sofort ein männliches Modell", antwortet dieser nach längerem Nachdenken und ohne jegliche Ironie. Dicrisio weiter: „Ihm stünde der *pretty-boy look* oder auch der verruchte *biker-Hollywood look*." Und: „Auf der Titelseite von *Vanity Fair* sähe er grossartig aus, etwa mit langem Haar, von der Windmaschine zerzaust, dem sinnlichen Ausdruck und einem romantischen Outfit." Sind dies die Figurationen Christi, die heute in die Modewelt hineinragen? So unwahrscheinlich dies klingt, Christus als Christian war bereits einmal Titelheld in *Vanity Fair*, nämlich im gleichnamigen Kapitel aus John Bunyans Welterfolg *Pilgrim's Progress* (1678).
  Zum festen Ablauf von Brunos Interviews gehört auch eine laufende Veränderung der Körperhaltung. Man redet zuerst stehend, dann sitzend und zuletzt liegend. Obwohl die auferlegte Struktur eher beklemmend denn *funky* wirkt, lehnt sich keiner der Befragten dagegen auf. Und im Liegen erreichen die Interviews jeweils ihren abschliessenden Tiefpunkt oder eben Höhepunkt der Peinlichkeit. Ein persönlicher Beitrag zu einer Wohltätigkeitsaktion (englisch *charity* oder lateinisch *caritas*), zur christlichen Nächstenliebe, soll geleistet werden:
  Bruno: „Unsere Show macht bei einer Wohltätigkeit *(charity)* mit, bei der es um taube oder

tote Kinder geht, wer weiss das schon, und ich wollte fragen, ob Du etwas für sie in die Kamera hinein tun kannst?"
Amer, der „trendsetter of stars", hebt die Arme hoch zu einer unverstandenen Geste, nachdem ihm Bruno erklärt, die tauben Kinder könnten seine verbale Nachricht nicht hören. Es vergehen unerträgliche Minuten des Schweigens. „That really makes a difference", kommentiert Bruno. Die Nächstenliebe stösst auch in der Episode mit Paul Wilmot, dem „god of seating plans", an ihre Schmerzgrenze. Für dieselbe *charity* soll Paul Wilmot wiederum taube Kinder in „sexual responsibility and safe sex" unterrichten. Nach einigen verbalen Fehlversuchen mimt Wilmot endlich eine Botschaft. Zum Zeichen des Neins winkt er mit dem Finger minutenlang in die Kamera. Offenbar wirkt die christliche Institution der *charity* so stark, dass die Absurdität der persönlichen Beiträge keinem der Beteiligten bewusst wird.

Politik machen

Kann Mode politische Akzente setzen, vielleicht sogar ein politisches Bewusstsein fördern? „Ja!", meint Shail Upadhya, Modedesigner an der New York Fashion Week 2004. Auf die Frage, worum es in seiner neusten Kollektion gehe, zeigt Upadhya politischen Willen: „Es sind *post 9-11* Kleider". Die an der Fashion Week gezeigte Mode sei noch „allzu sehr 10. September", er selbst hätte solche Kleider im Schrank gelassen, meint der Designer. Bruno, anstatt das Gesagte zu hinterfragen, denkt mit:
Bruno: „Warum legen wir nicht alle vor 9-11 getragenen Kleider auf einen riesigen Haufen, mieten einige Terroristen und jagen alles in die Luft?"
Upadhya: „Das ist eine grossartige Idee!"

Vielleicht ist es Brunos grosse Stärke, andere glauben zu lassen, sie hätten in ihm einen Verbündeten gefunden, jemanden, der mitdenkt und sich nicht scheut, Farbe zu bekennen. Vermutlich deshalb kommt Upadhya Brunos Aufforderung nach, „ein 12. September-Gesicht der Kamera zu zeigen". Er starrt unbewegt in die Kamera und meint, dies sei eine „unergründliche Miene" gewesen. „Und nun ein 10. September-Gesicht", fordert Bruno, worauf der Designer eine glückliche Miene macht. Und noch „ein 13. September-Gesicht" und jetzt noch „ein 14. September-Gesicht", fordert Bruno. Sichtlich genervt sucht Upadhya dennoch nach einem Gesichtsausdruck, dessen Sinn er aber nicht mehr versteht und dessen politische Performanz in der Ausdruckslosigkeit verschwindet. So zeigt die Mode ihr politisches Gesicht.

Das *Who's Who* des Identitätsschwindels

Gleich nebenan laufen die Vorbereitungen zur Frühlings- und Sommerkollektion von Caroline Herrera. „Wir haben ein kleines Problem. Wir kommen nicht an die Designerin Carolina Herrera heran", erklärt Bruno einer Dame aus dem Umfeld der Modeschau. „Könnten Sie sich als diese ausgeben?"
Unbekannte: „Woher kommen Sie?"
Bruno *(ihr ins Ohr flüsternd):* „Aus Österreich, dort haben sie keine Ahnung!"
Unbekannte: „Klar. Soll ich über die Kollektion reden?"
Bruno *(in die Kamera):* „Also, ich bin hier mit Carolina Herrera, mit der Designerin der ausgeflippten Show. Also, Carolina, wie läuft es denn?"
Hochstaplerin als Caroline Herrera: „Es war wundervoll. Dieses Jahr war meine Vision,

leger mit elegant zu verbinden, und wirklich, es war eine eklektische Mischung, sehr gegensätzlich."
Der Identitätschwindel fliegt auf einerseits, weil die Szene nicht geschnitten wird, andererseits, weil kurz darauf die echte Carolina Herrera interviewt wird. Solche Gesprächseröffnungen setzt Bruno mit Erfolg bei weniger bekannten Modemachern ein und stösst dabei auf keinerlei Scheu vor Hochstapelei. Um den Preis des 15-minütigen Ruhms sind alle bereit, eine Rolle zu spielen. Und erstaunlicherweise tun sie dies in Perfektion und auf Abruf. In der falschen Annahme, das Interview würde später geschnitten, erfüllen die Befragten gerne Brunos Erwartungen.
So auch Amer, Designer und Boutiquen-Besitzer an der Melrose Avenue, der gefragt wird, wie es war, als Madonna ins Geschäft kam. „Sie war nie hier", stellt er richtig. Nachdem Bruno ihm klarmacht, Madonna sei der Grund, weshalb das Interview stattfinde, nimmt Amer einen zweiten Anlauf auf dieselbe Frage:
Amer: „Es war wirklich erstaunlich."
Bruno: „Wieviele Kleidungsstücke hat sie gekauft?"
Amer: „Vierzehn."
Bruno: „Ist dies Madonnas Lieblingsgeschäft?"
Amer: „Ja."

Brunos Übertragung

Genau so wie Borat gibt auch Bruno keine Identifikationsfigur für die Massen ab. Er präsentiert im Gegensatz zu vielen anderen Fernsehmoderatoren keine tragfähige Alternative zur elitären Modewelt. Als Komiker ist seine Rolle vielmehr, die unbewussten Wünsche der Massen zum Ausdruck zu bringen und den Preis für die Übertretung selbst zu bezahlen bzw. auf die

Gesprächspartner abzuwälzen. Bruno bringt seine Gegenüber jeweils dazu, vor laufender Kamera Dinge zu sagen, welche der Zensur, dem Beichtgeheimnis oder der psychoanalytischen Schweigepflicht nicht hätten entgehen dürfen.

Tatsächlich stellt Bruno zu seinen Gesprächspartnern eine Übertragungsbeziehung in der Art der Psychoanalyse her. Alte Wünsche werden in seinem Beisein neu formuliert, d.h., in die Gegenwart übertragen, im Glauben, dass die persönliche Zensur durch den Schnitt der Kamera ersetzt würde. Seien dies nun faschistische Wünsche oder Identitätslügen, avantgardistische Sehnsüchte oder Christus-Phantasien, die Übertragung in die Gegenwart geschieht in Konkurrenz zu Bruno, der alles schon vormacht, und in Bezug auf die Kamera und das Mikrofon, von denen eine weltweite Übertragung erwartet wird. In dieser „lose-lose" Situation bleibt der erwartete Gewinn aus für die aufstrebenden Modemacher, für die Figur Brunos, der als aggressiver Rivale und Verlierer vorgezeichnet ist, und auch für die Modeindustrie in ihrem Verhältnis zum Konsumenten.

1 Gemäss einer Meldung vom November 2006 sollte Sacha Baron Cohen erneut vor Gericht gezogen werden. Die Anklage vertreten wollte wiederum der US-Anwalt Edward D. Fagan, der bereits jene Bewohner des rumänischen Dorfes Glod vertreten hatte, die sich in *Borat* (2006) des Inzests verdächtigt wähnten. „Der Grund für den Vorstoss: In *Bruno* soll Cohen eine Diffamierung Österreichs planen. Allein die Absicht so etwas tun zu wollen, reiche für eine Klage aus, so eine Vertraute von Anwalt Fagan. Sobald sich auch nur ein Österreicher in seinen Gefühlen verletzt sehe, könne eine Klage eingereicht werden. Laut Medienberichten sollen die Österreicher in *Bruno* als 'Lederhosen tragende Nazis' beschimpft werden." (www.firstnews.de, 29.11.2006)

2 Sämtliche Zitate entstammen den Episoden *Funkyzeit mit Bruno* von Sacha Baron Cohen und sind meine Übersetzungen. *Da Ali G Show: the Complete First Season*, New York: HBO Video, 2003. *Da Ali G Show: the Complete Second Season*, New York: HBO Video, 2005. *Ali G in da USAiii*, New York: HBO Video, 2005.

3 Zu Brunos Rolle gehört auch eine zur Schau getragene Homosexualität, mit der er sich Respekt und Zugehörigkeit zu einer latent homophilen Modeszene verschafft. Sie zeichnet sich stereotyp durch Begeisterung, Affektiertheit und Drang zur Selbstdarstellung aus, Eigenschaften eben, welche die internationale Modeszene spiegeln und mit denen Bruno diese an die Wand spielt.

4 Die doppelte Strategie erinnert auch an *Borat* (2006), wo Cohen die Rückständigkeit Kasachstans dazu benutzt, die Grundlagen der amerikanischen Gesellschaft blosszustellen.

5 Georg Simmel, *Philosophische Kultur*, Leipzig, 1911, S.32. Zit. nach Walter Benjamin, *Das Passagen-Werk, Gesammelte Schriften* V.1, Frankfurt/M.: Suhrkamp, 1982, S.127.

6 Eduard Fuchs, *Illustrierte Sittengeschichte vom Mittelater bis zur Gegenwart. Das bürgerliche Zeitalter. Ergänzungsband*, München, S.53–54. Zit. nach Walter Benjamin, *Passagen-Werk* V.1, Frankfurt/M.: Suhrkamp, 1982, S.128.

Verschwenderisch, mager, aber reich an Zeichen
Paris Hilton und die Mode

Daniela Janser

„Reichtum, Hintersinn und Grosszügigkeit sind von Willkür, Unbedarftheit und naturwüchsigem Zufall in Paris Hiltons Arbeit an sich selbst nicht mehr zu unterscheiden – wenn das nicht kritische Kunst ist, dann hat es sie nie gegeben."

–Dietmar Dath

Thorstein Veblen schreibt in seiner *Theory of the Leisure Class* (dt. *Theorie der feinen Leute*) ein schlankes Kapitel zum Thema „Dress as an Expression of the Pecuniary Culture" („Kleidung als Ausdruck des Geldes").[1] Das Buch erscheint 1899, Veblens Thesen beziehen sich also auf die Zeit vor der vorletzten Jahrhundertwende:

1. Kleider sind ein sehr sichtbares Zeichen von Wohlstand; das wichtigste Attribut dieser Kleider ist deshalb ihr Preis und ihre Exklusivität: sie sind auffällig verschwenderisch.

2. Diese Kleider müssen insbesondere auch klar machen, dass ihre Träger/innen keiner produktiven Arbeit nachgehen; sie sind deshalb

offensichtlich unpraktisch. Dies gilt nicht zuletzt für Frauenkleider. Das Korsett ist der Inbegriff der arbeitsverhindernden Unbequemlichkeit. Produktive Arbeit gilt für die *leisure class* eh als unanständig.

3. Die teuren Leisure-Kleider sind höchstens eine Saison lang zu tragen und damit immer auf dem neusten Stand; sie sind flüchtig. Überdies sind sie dem gemeinen Geschmack ein Gräuel und gelten nur als schön, weil sie gerade *in* und weil sie teuer sind.

Paris Hilton als *die* Ikone der neuen Leisure-Class nach der Jahrtausendwende scheint diese hundertjährigen Thesen auf den ersten Blick in allen Punkten zu bestätigen, mit nur kleinen Abweichungen. So ist das Korsett abgelöst worden durch eine rigorose Magerkeit – Ziel ist es, in die amerikanische Kleidergrösse 0 zu passen –, die aber natürlich ebenso ungesund und arbeitsverhindernd ist. Auch ist Hilton die ideale Reiche in Veblens Sinn, weil ihr – ursprüngliches – Vermögen geerbt ist, also mit keinerlei eigenen Verdiensten erarbeitet. Dass Hilton mit ihren Kleidern oft den „normalen Geschmack" beleidige und wie eine Hure aussehe – und auch wie eine solche fluche und lästere – bestätigt ihr das einfache Volk mit einer gewissen klassenkämpferisch angehauchten Genugtuung ebenfalls immer wieder gern.

Doch diese Übereinstimmungen sind natürlich nur die halbe Wahrheit. Paris Hilton macht deutlich, dass Veblens Thesen einen dialektischen Schritt weiter zu denken sind. Denn Leisure ist bei Paris Hilton keineswegs „süsses Nichtstun", sondern „harte Arbeit". Hergestellt wird nichts anderes als sie selbst: Die Schöpfung „Paris Hilton" entsteht in einer 24-stündigen aufwändigen Beschäftigung mit sich selbst und über die intensive Vermittlung durch die öffentliche, medialisierte Aufmerksamkeit. Das so

ständig neu erarbeitete Produkt Paris Hilton ist ein *professional socialite*. Man kann sie in dieser Funktion auch mieten, für Partys, Kluberöffnungen oder für den Wiener Opernball.

In seinem ursprünglich in der FAZ erschienen Artikel „Nackte, eine Treppe herunterpurzelnd" vergleicht Dietmar Dath zwei hauptberufliche Erbinnen aus verschiedenen Jahrhunderten: Peggy Guggenheim (die als Repräsentantin der Zeit Veblens gelten kann) und Paris Hilton als „Prototyp der Baureihe Fin de siècle 2.0".[2] Die eine, Guggenheim, ist als Kunstsammlerin und Förderern avantgardistischer Kunst in die Geschichte eingegangen, die andere, Hilton, inszeniert sich selbst konstant als Kunstwerk, oder genauer: als „Obszönitätsinstallation"[3]; als kritische Kunst, die ständig an sich arbeitet, wie Dath schreibt.

Das perfekte Fenster zu dieser Einsicht ist die Reality-Soap *The Simple Life* (2003 ff.). Sie ist das kleine Theater im grossen Theater mit dem Titel *Paris Hilton's Life of Leisure*. (Dass Hiltons Teilzeitfreundin Nicole Richie, die ihren Sidekick in *Simple Life* spielt, allgemein als „Bastard" bekannt ist – sie ist die adoptierte Tochter und Erbin des Soulstars Lionel Richie –, verleiht diesem Theater im Theater gar einen schwachen Shakespearschen Schimmer.) Genauso, wie Paris Hilton sich jeden Tag als superreiche Obszönitätsinstallation ihrer selbst erschafft und vorführt, spielen in der sehr erfolgreichen TV-Serie zwei Millionenerbinnen das „einfache Leben" als Parodie.

Welche Rolle spielen in diesem ineinander verschachtelten Theater die Kleider?

Paris Hilton spielt, verkauft und vermietet sich als eine Ware mit stets exklusiver Verpackung, sprich: Kleidung. Kein Kleid wird zweimal öffentlich vorgeführt, und kein Kleid, in welchem je eine andere Frau

fotografiert worden war, darf nochmals getragen werden. So lautet Hiltons selbstauferlegter Kodex, der einzige, an den sie sich konsequent hält. Damit wird die Mode zum allein Verlässlichen und Exklusiven in den sich endlos verflüchtigenden und reproduzierenden Loops von Leisure Class, Reality Show und Celebrity-Industrie. Die angestrebte Kleidergrösse 0 ist nie einfach ein Nullpunkt der Mode. Die Mode ist vielmehr das einzige Feld im Hilton-Universum, das stets ein bedeutsames Ereignis, eine aussagekräftige Markierung darstellt. „Ich war noch nie in China. Ich wusste nicht, was mich hier erwartet. Aber ich liebe die chinesische Mode", gab sie kürzlich – in ein hochgeschlossenes rotseidenes Chinamodezitaträcklein gekleidet – bei einem Besuch in Shanghai zu Protokoll.

Es erstaunt deshalb nicht, dass die Nachrichten des Zeichensystems Mode bei Hilton komplexer sind als das Meiste, was sie sonst von sich gibt. Im Pilotfilm zur ersten Staffel von *The Simple Life* gehen die beiden Heldinnen in Armeekleidern zum letzten Mal shoppen, bevor sie sich ans Ende der amerikanischen Welt fliegen lassen, um das Leben auf dem Bauernhof zu üben. Dort angekommen und zum ersten Mal in ihrem Leben zu „normaler Erwerbsarbeit" aufgeboten, tragen sie erneut militärische Tarnkleidung. So ergibt sich über die Kleiderwahl eine spekulative Identität zwischen den beiden Tätigkeiten: Shoppen ist Hiltons Äquivalent zur Arbeit. Und die Kleider sind ihr intellektuelles Ausdrucksmittel – nicht mehr, wie einst in Veblens Theorie, bloss Zeichen von Reichtum und Verschwendungssucht.

Hilton, die kein Kleid zweimal trägt und über ihre Fashion zeichenhaft kommuniziert, hat allerdings auch schon keine (speziellen) Kleider angezogen – und ist trotzdem aufgefallen. Zum ersten Mal in ihrem berüchtigten Sexvideo *One Night in Paris*, das als typischer Fall von absichtlicher Unabsichtlichkeit an die Öffentlichkeit gelangte. Zum zweiten Mal während ihres Gefängnisaufenthalts, von dem wir keine Bilder haben, ausser den gestellten ausgedachten Fotografien der britischen Künstlerin Alison Jackson, die in ihrem Fotoband *Confidential: What You See Is Not Real* neben vielen anderen Celebrities ein Hilton-Double hinter Gittern im orangen Häftlingsoverall oder nackt unter der Dusche inszeniert.[4] Das Pornovideo und der unsichtbare Gefängnisaufenthalt sind die beiden nackten Ausnahmen im Leben des millionenschweren Kleiderzeichenständers.

1 Thorstein Veblen, *Theorie der feinen Leute: Eine ökonomische Untersuchung der Institutionen*, Frankfurt/M.: Fischer, 2007.

2 Dietmar Dath, „Nackte, eine Treppe herunterpurzelnd: Peggy Guggenheim, Paris Hilton", in: *Heute keine Konferenz: Texte für die Zeitung*, Frankfurt/M.: Edition Suhrkamp, 2007, S. 278.

3 Dath, *Heute keine Konferenz*, S. 280.

4 Alison Jackson, *Confidential: What You See Is Not Real*, Hong Kong, Köln etc.: Taschen, 2007.

Learning from Louis Vuitton
Die Originalität der Fälschung

Aude Lehmann

„How true is it that you are what you wear?» fragt Bruno in seiner TV-Show *Funkyzeit with Bruno*. Ich hätte natürlich geantwortet: „Sehr." Aber was heisst das? Wie gehen wir damit um, dass die Kleider unser Sein bestimmen?

Sicherlich lieben wir die Mode, weil es uns ermöglicht, uns von anderen abzugrenzen und uns exklusiv zu fühlen. Ist es nicht ein Genuss, mit dem neusten Stück, das man irgendwo gefunden hat, herumzustolzieren, im sicheren Wissen, dass niemand anderes dasselbe tragen wird? (Noch sicherer kann man meist sein, dass niemand es genau so, in derselben Kombination, tragen wird.) Es macht Spass, sich für einen Moment als „Entdecker" zu fühlen, der aus einer Fülle von Vorschlägen etwas ganz Bestimmtes ausgewählt hat. Originalität, und sei es noch für einen so kurzen Moment, ist grossartig.

Ebenso aufregend kann es sein, zuerst zu beobachten, wie die anderen mit der Mode umgehen, und sich dann aufgrund dessen für etwas zu entscheiden. Denn egal, was jemand trägt, alle erzählen mit ihren Kleidern eine Geschichte, verkörpern eine bestimmte oder auch unbestimmte „Figur". Solche Beobachtungen mögen simpel und oberflächlich sein, und man könnte leicht daran kritisieren, dass es völlig unangebracht sei, Leute zu „katalogisieren". Aber ich finde es spannend, gerade die Oberflächlichkeit zu betrachten. Ich gehe mal davon aus, dass alle, die sich in irgendeiner Weise für Mode interessieren, oder besser gesagt, alle, denen es nicht ganz egal ist, was sie morgens anziehen, irgendwie auch bewusst damit umgehen, dass sie „etwas" oder „jemandem" mit ihrer Kleidung repräsentieren werden.

„Heute ziehe ich mich klassisch an. Oder sollte ich mal wieder meine roten Schuhe hervorholen? Das eventuell-doch-etwas-zu-farbige Foulard? Ist es ein Tag, um eleganter als gewöhnlich rumzulaufen? Wieso nicht mein Kleid tragen? Oder doch lieber casual, in Jeans?" Das heisst, dass die Darstellungen, die man von sich gibt, wandel- und steuerbar sind. Und wenn alle anderen auch wissen, dass „man ist, was man trägt" dann kann man damit sehr bewusst umgehen. Fast wie Schauspieler kann man seine Rolle spielen, oder auch eine fremde Rolle, auf die man gerade Lust hat.

Unter diesen Umständen beginnt die Mode wie ein Kostüm zu funktionieren, und sie kann wie ein Zitat verwendet werden. Man wird zu einer Figur, zum Bestandteil einer Geschichte, die weit über einen selbst hinausreicht. Und je unterschiedlicher die Leute sind, die sich eines bestimmten Kleidungsstücks, Accessoires oder „Styles" bedienen, desto spannender wird es, die Geschichte zu verfolgen. Die Kleidungsstücke werden komplexer, weil sie von den verschiedenen Trägern

– bzw. von den gespielten Rollen – mit immer neuen Bedeutungen aufgeladen werden, so dass die Bezüge und Verweise zwischen den Figuren schliesslich wichtiger sind als die einzelnen Outfits. Wenn man dann ein entsprechendes Kleidungsstück wählt, ist es nicht mehr möglich, sich ausserhalb der damit verbundenen Geschichte zu bewegen. Aber noch immer gibt es unzählige Möglichkeiten, sich zu differenzieren. Je nach dem, wie, wo und wann das Stück getragen wird, können neue, originelle Bezüge mit den anderen Trägern hergestellt werden – so wie innerhalb einer Geschichte ganz unterschiedliche Dialoge möglich sind.

Beispiele für solche grösseren, komplexen Geschichten gibt es viele: Jeans, T-Shirt, Sneakers … Es wäre völlig unglaubwürdig, sich als ersten Jeans-Träger präsentieren zu wollen. Viel glaubwürdiger ist es, sich mit seiner persönlichen Jeans einzigartig zu fühlen. Wenn alle mit eng geschnittenen Hosen herumlaufen, wäre es vielleicht wieder mal Zeit für *baggy*. Oder warum nicht an der nächsten Hochzeit, nachdem sämtliche Freundinnen schon Wochen im Voraus über ihre Abendkleider diskutierten, mit der hellblauen Lee aufkreuzen?

Noch interessanter wird die Geschichte, wenn etwas vergleichbares mit einem Label geschieht, denn im Gegensatz zu einem bestimmten Schnitt, einem Typ von Kleid oder Stoff verspricht das Label durch seine Signatur schon an sich eine gewisse Exklusivität. Wenn aber ein Logo von sehr vielen Leuten getragen wird, entsteht ein komplexes Zusammenspiel von Originalität und *being part of it*. Innerhalb einer Geschichte spielen dann viele verschiedene Figuren mit eigenen Hintergründen eine besondere und wichtige Rolle.

So war es in den letzten Jahren mit LV. Die Accessoires, die vorher eine bestimmte Zielgruppe definierten, waren plötzlich überall zu sehen. Es war wie eine riesige Bühne, auf der alle Platz hatten. Die Immer-schon-klassische-Mutter-Tochter-Enkelin-Kombo aus besserem Haus fand LV zwar langsam etwas langweilig, kaufte aber weiterhin beinahe jährlich das Multi-Format-Set der neuesten Kollektion. Die Schulfreundin der Enkelin erhielt nach langem Wünschen von ihrer ganzen Familie endlich auch eine kleine Handtasche zu Weihnachten geschenkt. 50Cent, wenig sparsam von Kopf bis Fuss in das LV Muster gekleidet, wurde noch immer ungern von der Verkäuferin bedient, weil er zu unbescheiden auftrat. Pharrell trug zu seinen Easy-Skater-bedruckten-funny-Shirts-aus-eigener-Kollektion ebenfalls gelegentlich eine diskrete LV-Mütze, und die ganze Teenager-Hip-Hop-Gang-vom-Schulhaus-nebenan leistete sich Accessoires – je nach Taschengeld – aus dem LV-Shop oder halt vom dubiosen Marktstand an der Chilbi. Der 35-jährige Szene-Graphic-Designer-Artist-DJ kaufte in NYC eine Es-gibt-sie-nur-100mal-Mütze, weil er natürlich auch Rap hört, aber meint, er hätte die wahren Zeiten des Hip-Hop durchlebt und könne zwischen Kunst und Kommerz unterscheiden. Die junge Fifty-studio-fifty-Mutter, die es immer noch geniesst, sich hie und da was „besonderes" für den Ausgang zu leisten, liess sich ebenso anstecken wie die afroamerikanische Familie – Mutter, Vater mit den beiden kleinen Söhnen –, die am Sonntag komplett mit LV-Mütze und/oder Tasche ausgestattet im Quartier flanierte. Das Werber-AD-CD-Team täuschte beim After-work-Whiskeysour kollektive Überraschung vor, als es entdeckte, dass alle denselben Geldbeutel hatten. Die Jetzt-schon-erfolgreiche-Künstlerin schliesslich, die sich für sehr gut angezogen hält ohne über Mode je ein Wort zu verlieren, überlegte lange hin und her, ob sie für die Vernissage auf die original Sixties-LV-Tasche ihrer Mutter zurückgreifen oder doch die Fake-LV-Tasche mit Klettverschluss von der letzte Sri Lanka-Reise tragen sollte.

Am Ende war es nicht mehr möglich, herauszufinden, wer da wen zitierte, wer wie wo angefangen hatte, und wer sich über wen lustig machte. Wer meinte es ernst, wer ironisch, wer trug ein Original, wer eine gute oder schlechte oder originelle Fälschung? Die Antwort ist nicht wichtig, denn alle spielten eine bedeutsame, je eigene Rolle, indem sie Teil der LV-Geschichte waren, die somit eine wunderbare Geschichte ist, um zu zeigen, dass wir *nicht* sind, was wir anziehen. Wie sonst wäre es möglich, dass so viele unterschiedliche Leute plötzlich dasselbe tragen?

Ghetto Fabulous
Blackface-Maskerade von der Minstrel Show zum Hip-Hop

Susanne von Ledebur

Kurz nachdem sein Film *Bamboozled* (2000) erschien, traf Regisseur Spike Lee eines Morgens, als er seine Tochter zur Schule brachte, Tommy Hilfiger. „Wie konntest du mir das antun?", habe Hilfiger ihn jammernd gefragt, „mir, der ich doch immer in den Martin Luther King-Fonds einzahle und für die Sommerlager für Ghetto-Kinder spende?"[1] Hilfigers Klage bezog sich auf einen erfundenen Werbespot, den Spike Lee in seinen Film eingebaut hatte. „Timmy, Timmy, Timmy", rufen darin Frauen in knappem Hilfiger Outfit. „Hilniger" rappt eine Gang Männer in Hilfiger-Hoodies zurück. Mitten in der Gruppe steht ein Mann, der aussieht wie Tommy Hilfiger, und gibt Werbe-Parolen zum besten: „Just stay in the Ghettto! Stay broke!"

Mit diesem Werbespot-Witz unterstellte Spike Lee Hilfiger und anderen (weissen) Herstellern von Hip-Hop-Outfits (wie Adidas beispielsweise) aber nicht nur, dass sie das Ghetto- und Gangsterdasein verherrlichten, sondern er brachte sie auch in die Nähe der Minstrel Show. Der Werbespot erscheint im Vorprogramm der *New Millennium Minstrel Show*, die vom Helden des Films, dem afroamerikanischen TV-Produzenten Pierre Delacroix, entwickelt wird. Delacroix versucht, mit einer möglicht dummen und rassistischen Sendung über Schwarze seine Entlassung zu provozieren, und verfolgt damit eine ähnliche Strategie wie die jüdischen Theaterproduzenten in Mel Brooks' berühmtem Broadway-Stück (und Film) *The Producers,* die mit einem vermeintlich sicheren Flop, dem anti-

semitischen Musical *Springtime for Hitler,* bei der Versicherung Geld abstauben wollen. Der Witz in beiden Fällen ist selbstverständlich, dass die Stücke grosse Erfolge feiern, obwohl oder gerade weil sie antisemitisch bzw. rassistisch sind.

Zwar sind in Delacroix' Show für das neuen Millennium alle Darsteller schwarz, doch treten sie wie die vorwiegend weissen Darsteller der Minstrel Shows aus dem 19. Jahrhundert in „Blackface" auf: in russschwarz angemaltem Gesicht, mit überzeichnetem rotem Mund, einer Wollperücke und clownesken Clochard-Kleidern. Solche Maskierungen, die das afroamerikanische Aussehen ins Groteske und Lächerliche verzerren, entstanden 1820 im Norden der USA – vor allem in New York – und erfreuten sich grosser Beliebtheit bei einem vornehmlich weissen Unterschichts-Publikum. Die Blackface-Figuren waren oft heimatlose, ewig wandernde, arme Schlucker, die zu Banjo in einem künstlichen Schwarzen-Slang über ihre Missgeschicke sangen und dazu tanzten. Einer der berühmtesten war der vom weissen Schauspieler Thomas Dartmouth Rice erfundene und personifizierte Jim Crow. Er war – vor allem zu Beginn – eine dichte, mehrdeutige Figur, die Opfer und Täter zugleich war und sich über bekannte Autoritäten und sich selbst lustig machte. Besonderes Aufsehen erregte er durch seine Tanzweise, eine Variation jener Tänze, die in den Häfen New Yorks von Afro-Amerikanern tatsächlich aufgeführt wurden.

In den 1840er-Jahren wurden Blackface-Auftritte mit den Minstrel Shows zur vollen Abendvorstellung ausgebaut und die Blackface-Figuren standardisiert. Es gab nun ein festes Set von Figuren. Aus Jim Crow wurden Bones und Tambo, nach ihren Instrumenten benannte, höchst musikalische Figuren, zugleich aber dumm, faul und ungezogen (vergleichbar vielleicht mit Harpo bei den Marx Brothers). Kontrastiert wurden sie vom so genannten *interlocutor*, der als *master of ceremony* auftrat und ein eloquentes, aristokratisches Englisch sprach (hier sieht man Parallelen zu Groucho Marx). Am Anfang der Minstrel Show stand meist ein Dialog des *interlocutors* mit Tambo und Bones, wobei der Witz daraus resultierte, dass die beiden Dummköpfe die geschwollene Rede nicht begriffen. Weitere Figuren waren Old Uncle und Old Auntie, zwei ihrem Sklavenhalter treu ergebene Diener, sowie der Dandy, ein städtischer, freier Schwarzer, der über seinen Verhältnissen lebt und die Sprache und Umgangsform der weissen Oberschicht nachahmt und parodiert.

Aus diesen Stereotypen entwickelten sich im Verlauf der Jahrzehnte zahllose clowneske, rassistische Maskottchen, Ikonen und Markennamen, wovon die meisten spätestens in den 1950er-Jahren wieder verschwanden, als die schwarze Bürgerrechtsbewegung an Einfluss gewann. Unter denen, die heute noch existieren, stellt beispielsweise Uncle Ben vom gleichnamigen Reis eine Fortführung des

Old Uncle dar, und die in den USA weit verbreitete Marke für Pancakes Fertigprodukte, „Aunt Jemima", ist ein Ableger der Old Auntie. Aber auch in den Cartoons hielt das rassistische Stereotyp des ungebildeten, immer fröhlichen, musikalischen Schwarzen Einzug. Walt Disney erfand in den späten 1920ern seinen Mickey Mouse als einen Minstrel-Show-Charakter. Mickey sieht mit den weissen Handschuhen nicht nur aus wie ein Blackface-Schauspieler, in der frühen Version tanzt und singt er auch und ist geradezu blödsinnig gut gelaunt.

Die Minstrel Show war die erste genuin amerikanische Theaterform und wohl ein Vorbild für diverse grossartige Auftrittsformen von heute. Beispielsweise ist die so genannte *stump speech* – ein Monolog über irgendein Thema von Politik über Wissenschaft bis zum neuesten Klatsch, den Bones bzw. Tambo auf einem Baumstumpf stehend hielten –, ein klarer Vorläufer der heutigen Stand-up-Comedians. Zudem war die Minstrel Show für afroamerikanische Sänger und Schauspieler lange Zeit *das* Tor zum Showbusiness und zur Berühmtheit. Doch seit 1950 ist wohl keine andere Aufführungsform so verpönt wie sie. „Eine Komödie über Sklaverei", fasst Spike Lee sein Urteil zusammen, „ungefähr so lustig wie eine Komödie über den Holocaust."

Kein Wunder also, war Tommy Hilfiger nicht glücklich, dass Lee in *Bamboozled* einen Timmy Hilniger als Sponsor der *New Millennium Minstrel Show* präsentierte. Es war ein klares Statement gegen den Designer – und auch gegen die Hip-Hopper, die seine Kleider tragen. Für Spike Lee ist, wie er in einem Kommentar explizit erklärte, „der Gangsta-Rap nichts anderes als die Minstrel Show des 20. Jahrhunderts." Obwohl Lee diesen Bezug nicht weiter ausführte, kann man

ihn sich spielend ausmalen. Der Gangsta-Look oder *ghetto fabulous style* – wie ihn P. Diddy nannte – kann als neue Form der Dandy-Figur aus der Minstrel Show verstanden werden. Tatsächlich war Spike Lees Vergleich nicht neu. Der afroamerikanische Jazzkritiker Stanley Crouch beispielsweise hatte immer wieder auf die Parallele hingewiesen. Der Erfolg der Minstrel Shows habe darauf beruht, dass das rassistische Stereotyp vom faulen, kriminellen Schwarzen bestätigt wurde – der z.B. Hühner und Wassermelonen klaut –, und ebenso würden heutige Rapper dadurch berühmt, dass sie angebliche Lebensweisen der Schwarzen wie Promiskuität und Gangsterdasein verkörperten.[2]

Vergleichbar hatte der amerikanische Literaturwissenschaftler W.T. Lhamon Jr. aufgezeigt, dass M.C. Hammer im Video zu *Hammer Time* (1990) exakt jenen Tanz vollführt, der in den Häfen von New York um 1820 populär war und den T.D. Rice für seine Jim Crow Figur übernahm.[3] Allerdings hatte Lhamon im Gegensatz zu Lee oder Crouch diese Parallele nicht zu dem Zweck gezogen, M.C. Hammer zu denunzieren oder kritisieren. Im Gegenteil: In seiner Untersuchung der frühen Blackface-Aufführungen wie beispielsweise *Jim Crow* entdeckt Lhamon nicht nur rassistische Töne. Zum einen weist er darauf hin, dass die Blackface-Darsteller in Gegenden aufgetreten sind, in denen eine weisse und schwarze Unterschicht zusammenlebte, beispielsweise im siebten Bezirk New Yorks. Dort tanzten in den 1820er Jahren Afroamerikaner im M.C. Hammer-Stil auf dem Fischmarkt Catherine, am selben Ort, an dem hundert Jahre zuvor die Teilnehmer jenes Aufstands hingerichtet worden waren, der als „Negroe Revolt" in die Geschichte einging, obwohl spanische, irische und eng-

lische Immigranten daran ebenso beteiligt waren wie Afroamerikaner.

Vor diesem Hintergrund versteht Lhamon Blackface als kulturelle Ausdrucksform einer ethnisch durchmischten Unterschicht. Er macht in den frühen Blackface-Inszenierungen eine grosse Faszination der weissen Schauspieler für „schwarze" Gesten und Ausdrucksweisen aus, und betont, dass die Witze häufig nicht nur auf den „schwarzen" Sprecher selbst zielten, sondern zugleich gegen bekannte Autoritäten gerichtet waren. Das Publikum lachte nicht nur über die Blackfaces, sondern identifizierte sich auch mit ihnen. Es bestand aus jungen Arbeitern, irischen, französischen, deutschen, englischen Immigranten, aber auch Afro-Amerikanern, die sich mit den Missgeschicken und der gesellschaftlichen Ausgrenzung eines Jim Crow und später eines Bone und Tambo identifizieren konnten. So war Blackface, bevor es in den 1850ern in krude Typisierungen erstarrte, Teil einer proletarischen Jugendkultur und bezog seine Anziehungskraft über eine gewisse *street credibility*. Figuren wie Jim Crow wurden unter anderem auch deshalb so beliebt, weil sie die Aura des Aussenstehenden, des Widerständigen hatten.

Dem entspricht, dass den Songs und Witzen der Blackfaces oft ein reflexives Moment eigen war. In einer berühmten Nummer machte sich T.D. Rice als Jim Crow einerseits über die Weissen lustig, die meinen, mit angemaltem Gesicht Schwarze darstellen zu können, und beklagte sich andererseits darüber, dass er diese Dilettanten nicht mal anschauen gehen kann, weil in besagtem Theater keine Schwarzen eingelassen werden. Ohne zu verneinen, dass die Blackfaces immer auch rassistisch waren, gelingt es Lhamon anhand solcher Songs, noch ganz andere Facetten herauszustellen und ein insgesamt schillerndes Bild der Minstrel Shows zu zeichnen.

Insofern hätte Spike Lee mit seiner Behauptung zwar recht, dass die heutigen Gangsta-Rapper die Tradition der Blackfaces fortführten, weniger jedoch mit der Annahme, dass dabei bloss eine rassistische Ikonographie übernommen werde. Natürlich kann man die in den letzten Jahren im Hip-Hop zentral gewordene Figur des Pimp, des Zuhälters, als perfekte Reinkarnation des rassistischen Vorurteils sehen, dass Schwarze promisk und kriminell seien. Aber lachen wir beispielsweise in Snoop Doggs TV-Show *Doggy Fizzle Televizzle* tatsächlich über den sich als Pimp gebenden Snoop? Oder wird nicht spätestens bei Snoops Besuch bei Hugh Hefner deutlich, wer der

wirkliche Zuhälter ist und wer die gekonnte Parodie davon?

Letztlich weiss auch Spike Lee um die Vielschichtigkeit der Blackface-Tradition. Entgegen seinem expliziten Kommentar zum Film sind die kurzen Ausschnitte aus Delacroix' *New Millennium Minstrel Show* bisweilen richtig lustig. Lee konnte für die Rolle des Sleep'n' Eat, eines Charakters der Show, den bekannten schwarzen *comedian* Tommy Davidson gewinnen, und eine der Nummern enstammt denn auch dessen Programm. Direkt bei der Tradition der Minstrel Show bediente sich Spike Lee aber für seine Hauptfigur. Pierre Delacroix, der in einem künstlichen englischen Akzent und mit ungeheurer Eloquenz spricht, ist offensichtlich dem klassischen *interlocutor* nachgezeichnet. Während Spike Lee in

Bamboozled also die rassistischen Tendenzen der Minstrel Show herausstreicht, ist sein Film selber eine. *Bamboozled* bewahrt damit die ganze schillernde Ambivalenz, die der Minstrel Show eigen war und die viele heutige Inszenierungen der Gangsta-Rapper und Hip-Hopper noch immer auszeichnet.

1 Alle Zitate von Spike Lee stammen aus dem „Audio-Kommentar mit Regisseur Spike Lee" auf der *Bamboozled*-DVD, New Line Home Video, USA 2001.

2 Zit. nach Jonathan Fischer, „Ein Mann sieht schwarz: ‚Public Enemies‘, Flavor Flav und die Rückkehr rassistischer Klischees in den Pop", in: *Süddeutsche Zeitung*, 24.11.2007.

3 W.T. Lhamon Jr., *Raising Cain: Blackface Performance from Jim Crow to Hip Hop*, Cambridge, MA: Harvard UP 1998.

Da Gucci, da Fendi, da Prada
50 Cents höchst auffälliger Konsum

Tan Wälchli

Seit dem Aufstieg der Gangsta-Rapper ist der Hip-Hop zugleich erfolgreicher und schlechter angesehen als je zuvor. Während Jay-Z, 50 Cent, P. Diddy, Snoop Dogg u. a. weltweit Millionen von Alben verkaufen, beklagt eine anspruchsvollere Hörerschaft die Kommerzialisierung und die Banalität der Texte. Früher, so heisst es, sei alles besser gewesen: Der Hip-Hop sei als Subkultur einer benachteiligten Gesellschaftsschicht entstanden und habe politisch-subversive Inhalte vertreten. Ebenso treffend wie witzig wurde diese Stimmung anlässlich der MTV-Awards 2006 in

New York von 50 Cent wiedergegeben. Auf seine Chancen angesprochen, einen Preis zu gewinnen, antwortete er: „I usually don't get the awards I'm supposed to, but I always get my cheque."

Die Fixierung aufs Geld kommt besonders deutlich zum Ausdruck, wenn sich Jay-Z oder Diddy als „Entrepreneurs" bezeichnen und Firmenkonglomerate aufbauen, zu denen neben den Plattenlabels auch Beteiligungen am Film- und Fernsehgeschäft, eigene Kleiderlinien, Restaurants u. a. gehören. Als Vorbilder dienen dabei jene beinahe mythischen Self-Made-Men

wie Rockefeller, die als der perfekte Ausdruck des „American Dream" gelten. An dieser gesellschaftlichen Elite orientiert sich auch der Kleider- und Lifestyle der Gangsta-Rapper: Sie tragen mit Vorliebe teure Anzüge – „da Gucci, da Fendi, da Prada", wie 50 Cent in einem seiner Hits, *P.I.M.P.* (2003), rappte – und geben Unmengen von Geld für Autos, Jachten, Villen und glamouröse Parties aus. Allerdings ist das Verhältnis zu den Vorbildern wie Rockefeller nicht ganz ungetrübt. Wenn beispielsweise Jay-Z sein Kleiderlabel *Rock A Fella* nennt, ist der parodistische Ton nicht zu überhören. Und wenn Snoop Porno-Videos produziert oder so banale Produkte wie Grill-Accessoires vertreibt, erleidet das Bild des grossen Entrepreneurs heftige Kratzer.

Die Kluft, die sich hier auftut, ist grösser, als es auf den ersten Blick manchmal scheint. Denn obwohl sich die Gangsta-Rapper als amerikanische Self-Made-Unternehmer geben, sind sie noch lange nicht zur gesellschaftlichen Elite aufgestiegen. Nicht einmal von den Luxusgüter-Herstellern, deren Kunden sie sind, werden sie akzeptiert. Beispielsweise erhielt noch kein Gangsta-Rapper entsprechende Werbe-Verträge angeboten, und äusserst selten gibt es in Mode-Magazinen Fotostrecken, in denen Hip-Hopper auftreten. Auch ist bekannt, dass man bei Gucci wenig Freude hat, wenn P. Diddy mit seiner Crew stundenlang den Mailänder Flagship-Store belegt. Obwohl es meist nicht öffentlich gesagt wird, ist die Angst gross, dass solche Eskapaden gewisse Teile der etablierten Kundschaft abschrecken könnten, und in einem Fall führten diese Überlegungen sogar zu einem handfesten Skandal. Als sich im Sommer 2006 der CEO des Champanger-Herstellers Roederer öffentlich darüber beschwerte, dass die Edelmarke des Hauses, Cristal, durch den exzessiven Konsum der Hip-Hopper an Ansehen verloren habe, reagierte Jay-Z beleidigt, sprach von Rassismus und verbannte den Namen Cristal aus seinen Lyrics und Bars.

Doch dürfte es zweifelhaft bleiben, ob sich das Problem, wie Jay-Z meinte, mit einer anderen Champagner-Marke lösen lässt. Denn die Art und Weise, wie die Gangsta-Rapper den glamourösen Lifestyle zelebrieren, passt schlicht nicht zum hergebrachten Image der Edel-Marken. Die Hip-Hopper konsumieren nämlich „zu viel des Guten", egal ob es sich um Kleider, Alkohol,

Schmuck, Autos oder Wohnungseinrichtungen handelt. Dies wird von der herrschenden Klasse als stillos wahrgenommen und mit der fehlenden Bildung und „Kultur" der Gangsta-Rapper erklärt. Sie haben nie gelernt, was Stil ist und wie man mit Luxusgütern umgeht. Und damit drängt sich die Frage auf, wie sie zu ihrem Reichtum gelangt sind. Denn wie sollte man ohne Bildung so viel Geld verdienen? Und wie, wenn einem offenkundig jedes Verständnis für die wahren Werte von Markenprodukten abgeht; wenn man also die Grundlagen des Kapitalismus nicht verstanden hat? Offenbar, so lautet der nahe liegende Schluss, ist beim Verdienst der Rapper nicht alles mit rechten Dingen zugegangen.

Dieser Verdacht ist es, der die Hip-Hop-Entrepreneurs eng mit den Gangstern verbindet. Und macht sich nicht auch in beiden Fällen dieselbe Obsession mit Luxus-Gütern bemerkbar? So jedenfalls zeigt es Jim Sheridan in seinem Biopic über 50 Cent, *Get Rich or Die Trying* (2005). In dem Film, der die Drogendealer-Karriere des jugendlichen 50 schildert, erscheinen die Luxusgüter als die erträumten, unerreichbaren Statussymbole der Ghetto-Kids. Sein erstes Honorar investiert der kleine 50 in ein paar weisse Sneakers, die er schon lange im Schaufenster eines Ladens gesehen hatte, und wenige Jahre später wird dank des Crack-Booms der lang gehegte Traum vom weissen S-Klasse-Mercedes wahr. An dieser auf Konsum fixierten Weltsicht ändert sich auch nichts, als 50 kurz darauf wegen Konflikten in der Gang ins Abseits gerät und, zum Aussteigen gezwungen, mit Rappen beginnt. Weit davon entfernt, damit eine Bekehrung oder einen sozialen Aufstieg zu vollziehen, lebt er weiterhin im Ghetto und frönt dem Gangsta-Style. So besehen wird der eigentliche

Grund für die Ablehnung verständlich, die den Gangsta-Rappern entgegengebracht wird. Während von fehlender „Kultur" und vom stillosem Umgang mit Luxusgütern die Rede ist, geht es eigentlich um das Problem, dass der Reichtum nicht „mit rechten Mitteln" erworben wurde. Und diesbezüglich macht die herrschende Klasse offenbar keinen Unterschied zwischen Dealern und Rappern – Rauschmittel und Hip-Hop sind gleichermassen verpönte Konsumgüter, und wer sie verkauft, wird mit gesellschaftlicher Ächtung bestraft.

Das aber heisst, dass sich andererseits der masslose Umgang, den die Gangsta-Rapper mit Kleidern, Champagner, Autos, etc. pflegen, als eine Inszenierung verstehen lässt: Durch das *bewusst* „stillosen" Konsum betonen die Rapper, dass sie – wegen ihrer Berufe – niemals dazu gehören werden, egal wie reich sie sind. Sie entlarven die Statussymbole, mit denen sich die gesellschaftliche Elite abgrenzt, als Verdinglichung von leeren Versprechen. So lässt sich der Gangsta-Hip-Hop als eine höchst politische Bewegung verstehen –, wobei hier der Mode- und Lifestyle das eigentliche Ausdrucksmittel des Politischen ist. Indem sie in „stilloser" Weise „zuviel des Guten" konsumieren, machen die Rapper den „amerikanische Traum" vom Self-Made-Man – vom sozialen Aufstieg für alle – als ein falsches Versprechen erkenntlich:

Edition for Whyart

Lex Trueb in collaboration
with Mathieu Meyer

Whyart Donkey (green)
Spring / Summer 2009
Clay, burned and glazed
33 × 29 × 21 cm
Edition of 1
EUR 230.—

All Donkeys come with a
reproduction of *A La Mode*
in the form of a magazine
Edition of 6
20.5 × 30 cm

Whyart Donkey (white)
Autumn/Winter 2009
Clay, burned and glazed
33×29×19 cm
Edition of 1
EUR 220.—

The original version of the Isokon Penguin Donkey Bookcase was designed by Egon Riss in 1939 to hold Penguin books. It was named the Donkey because it had four legs and two panniers. The space between the side-compartments could be used for magazines. The shelves in the bookcase were just the right size to house the distinctive orange-covered Penguin paperbacks. Shortly after the Donkey had been launched, the Second World War broke out, and both the publication of Penguin books and the production of the Donkey were ceased. Only about a hundred Donkeys had been made.

Whyart Donkey (yellow)
Spring/Summer 2009
33×27×22 cm
Edition of 1
EUR 220.—

Whyart Donkey (grey)
Autumn/Winter 2009
32×28×21 cm
Edition of 1
EUR 240.—

Whyart Donkey (red)
Spring/Summer 2009
32×29×19 cm
Edition of 1
EUR 190.—

Whyart Donkey (blue)
Autumn/Winter 2009
34×24×20 cm
Edition of 1
EUR 240.—

For further information please contact
www.bookhorse.ch

This publication has received
generous support from:
Swiss Federal Office of Culture
Präsidialdepartement der Stadt Zürich
Migros Kulturprozent
Fachstelle Kultur Kanton Zürich

 BUNDESAMT FÜR KULTUR
OFFICE FÉDÉRAL DE LA CULTURE
UFFICIO FEDERALE DELLA CULTURA
UFFIZI FEDERAL DA CULTURA